Bond
No.1 for exam success

English
Assessment Papers
9–10 years
Book 2

OXFORD
UNIVERSITY PRESS

OXFORD
UNIVERSITY PRESS

Great Clarendon Street, Oxford, OX2 6DP, United Kingdom

Oxford University Press is a department of the University of Oxford.
It furthers the University's objective of excellence in research, scholarship,
and education by publishing worldwide. Oxford is a registered trade mark of
Oxford University Press in the UK and in certain other countries

The manufacturer's authorised representative in the EU for product safety is Oxford University Press España S.A. of el Parque Empresarial San Fernando de Henares, Avenida de Castilla, 2 – 28830 Madrid (www.oup.es/en).

Text © Sarah Lindsay 2015
Illustrations © Oxford University Press 2015

The moral rights of the authors have been asserted

First published in 2015

This new edition 2020

All rights reserved. No part of this publication may be reproduced, stored in a retrieval system, or transmitted, in any form or by any means, without the prior permission in writing of Oxford University Press, or as expressly permitted by law, by licence or under terms agreed with the appropriate reprographics rights organization. Enquiries concerning reproduction outside the scope of the above should be sent to the Rights Department, Oxford University Press, at the address above.

You must not circulate this work in any other form and you must impose this same condition on any acquirer

British Library Cataloguing in Publication Data
Data available

978-0-19-277738-6

10 9

Paper used in the production of this book is a natural, recyclable product made from wood grown in sustainable forests.
The manufacturing process conforms to the environmental regulations of the country of origin.

Printed in China

Acknowledgements

The publishers would like to thank the following for permissions to use copyright material:

Page make-up: OKS Prepress, India
Illustrations: Lisa Smith (Sylvie Poggio Artists Agency)
Cover illustrations: Lo Cole

P2 'You Can't Be That' from *Thawing Frozen Frogs* by Brian Patten, copyright © Brian Patten, 1990. Reproduced by permission of the author; p7 extract from *A Pack of Liars* by Anne Fine, copyright © Anne Fine, 1988. Published by Penguin Ltd, reprinted by permission of David Higham Associates; p12 extract from *How to run a marathon*, by Cathy Shipton and Liz McColgan copyright © Cathy Shipton and Liz McColgan 1997. Reprinted by permission of HarperCollins Publishers Ltd; p23 extract from *Questions and Answers: Oceans and Rivers* by Barbara Taylor © Kingfisher Publications Plc 2000. Reproduced by permission of the publisher, all rights reserved; p29 extract from *War Horse* by Michael Morpurgo, copyright © 1990 Michael Morpurgo. Published by Egmont UK Ltd London and used with permission; p41 extract from *Plan* UK leaflet; reproduced by permission of Plan UK; p46 extract from *The Voyage of the Dawn Treader* by C S Lewis copyright © C S Lewis Pte Ltd 1952. Extract reprinted by permission; pp52–53 extract from *Wordly Wise* by Barrie Wade, Ann Wade and Maggie Moore, Storychest 1986; p58 extract from 'Polar explorer brought in from the cold after 38 years' by Esther Adley, 17 October 2006. Copyright © Guardian News and Media Limited 2007.

Although we have made every effort to trace and contact all copyright holders before publication this has not been possible in all cases. If notified, the publisher will rectify any errors or omissions at the earliest opportunity.

Links to third party websites are provided by Oxford in good faith and for information only. Oxford disclaims any responsibility for the materials contained in any third party website referenced in this work.

Before you get started

What is Bond?

This book is part of the Bond Assessment Papers series for English, which provides **thorough and continuous practice of key English skills** from ages five to thirteen. Bond's English resources are ideal preparation for Key Stage 1 and Key Stage 2 SATs, the 11+ and other selective school entrance exams.

What does this book cover and how can it be used to prepare for exams?

English 9–10 years Book 1 and *Book 2* can be used both for general practice and as part of the run up to 11+ exams, Key Stage 2 SATs and other selective exams. The papers practise comprehension, spelling, grammar and vocabulary work. The coverage is also matched to the National Curriculum and the National Literacy Strategy. It is outside the scope of this book to practise extended and creative writing skills. *Bond Focus on Writing* provides full coverage of writing skills.

What does the book contain?

- **12 papers** – each one contains 100 questions.
- **Tutorial links throughout** – 📖 – this icon appears in the margin next to the questions. It indicates links to the relevant section in *How to do 11+ English*, our invaluable subject guide that offers explanations and practice for all core question types.
- **Scoring devices** – there are score boxes in the margins and a Progress Chart on page 68. The chart is a visual and motivating way for children to see how they are doing. It also turns the score into a percentage that can help decide what to do next.
- **Next Steps Planner** – advice on what to do after finishing the papers can be found on the inside back cover.
- **Answers** – located in an easily-removed central pull-out section.

How can you use this book?

One of the great strengths of Bond Assessment Papers is their flexibility. They can be used at home, in school and by tutors to:

- set **timed formal practice** tests – allow about 45 minutes per paper. Reduce the suggested time limit by five minutes to practise working at speed.

- provide **bite-sized chunks** for regular practice
- **highlight strengths and weaknesses** in the core skills
- identify **individual needs**
- set **homework**
- follow a **complete 11+ preparation strategy** alongside *The Parents' Guide to the 11+* (see below).

It is best to start at the beginning and work though the papers in order. If you are using the book as part of a careful run-in to the 11+, we suggest that you also have four other essential Bond resources close at hand:

Bond 11+ English Handbook: the subject guide that explains all the question types practised in this book. Use the cross-reference icons to find the relevant sections.

Focus on Comprehension: the practical handbook that clearly shows children how to read and understand the text, understand the questions and assess their own answers.

Focus on Writing: the essential resource that explains the key components of successful writing.

The Parents' Guide to the 11+: the step-by-step guide to the whole 11+ experience. It clearly explains the 11+ process, provides guidance on how to assess children, helps you to set complete action plans for practice and explains how you can use *English 9–10 years Book 1* and *Book 2* as part of a strategic run-in to the exam.

See the inside front cover for more details of these books.

What does a score mean and how can it be improved?

It is unfortunately impossible to predict how a child will perform when it comes to the 11+ (or similar) exam if they achieve a certain score on any practice book or paper. Success on the day depends on a host of factors, including the scores of the other children sitting the test. However, we can give some guidance on what a score indicates and how to improve it.

If children colour in the Progress Chart on page 68, this will give an idea of present performance in percentage terms. The Next Steps Planner inside the back cover will help you to decide what to do next to help a child progress. It is always valuable to go over wrong answers with children. If they are having trouble with any particular question type, follow the tutorial links to *How to do 11+ English* for step-by-step explanations and further practice.

Don't forget the website…!

Visit www.bond11plus.co.uk for lots of advice, information and suggestions on everything to do with Bond, the 11+ and helping children to do their best.

Key words

Some special words are used in this book. You will find them in **bold** each time they appear in the Papers. These words are explained here.

abbreviation	a word or words which are shortened
abstract noun	a word referring to a concept or idea *love*
acronym	a word or letter string made up from the initial letters of other words
adjectival phrase	a group of words describing a noun
adjective	a word that describes somebody or something
adverb	a word that gives extra meaning to a verb
alphabetical order	words arranged in the order found in the alphabet
antonym	a word with a meaning opposite to another word *hot – cold*
clause	a section of a sentence with a verb
collective noun	a word referring to a group *swarm*
compound word	a word made up of two other words *football*
conjunction	a word used to link sentences, phrases or words *and, but*
connective	a word or words that join clauses or sentences
contraction	two words shortened into one with an apostrophe placed where the letter/s have been dropped *do not = don't*
definition	a meaning of a word
dialect	regional variation of vocabulary in the spoken language
diminutive	a word implying smallness *booklet*
homophone	a word that has the same sound as another but a different meaning or spelling *right/write*
indirect speech	(also known as reported speech) what has been said without using the exact words or inverted commas
metaphor	an expression in which something is described in terms usually associated with another *the sky is a sapphire sea*
modal verb	a verb that changes the meaning of other verbs, for example *can, will*
noun	a word for somebody or something
onomatopoeic	a word that echoes a sound associated with its meaning *hiss*
parenthesis	this is a word or phrase that is separated off from the main sentence by brackets, commas or dashes usually because it contains additional information not essential to its understanding
past tense	form of a verb showing something that has already happened
personal pronoun	a pronoun used when writing about ourselves *I, you*
phrase	a group of words that act as a unit
plural	more than one *cats*
possessive pronoun	a pronoun showing to whom something belongs *mine, ours, his, hers, yours, theirs*
prefix	a group of letters added to the beginning of a word *un, dis*
preposition	a word that relates other words to each other – *he sat behind me, the book on the table*
present tense	form of a verb showing something happening now
pronoun	a word used to replace a noun
relative clause	a special type of clause that makes the meaning of a noun more specific, for example *The prize that I won was a book*
proper noun	the names of people, places etc. *Ben*
root word	a word to which prefixes or suffixes can be added to make another word *quickly*
singular	one *cat*
suffix	a group of letters added to the end of a word *ly, ful*
synonym	a word with the same or very similar meaning to another word *quick – fast*
verb	a 'doing' or 'being' word

Paper 1

You Can't Be That

I told them:
When I grow up
I'm not going to be a scientist
Or someone who reads the news on TV.
No, a million birds will fly through me. 5
I'M GOING TO BE A TREE!

They said,
You can't be that. No, you can't be that.

I told them:
When I grow up 10
I'm not going to be an airline pilot,
A dancer, a lawyer or an MC.
No, huge whales will swim in me.
I'M GOING TO BE AN OCEAN!

They said, 15
You can't be that. No, you can't be that.

I told them:
I'm not going to be a DJ,
A computer programmer, a musician or beautician.
No, streams will flow through me, 20
I'll be the home of eagles;
I'll be full of nooks, crannies, valleys and fountains.
I'M GOING TO BE A RANGE OF MOUNTAINS!

They said,
You can't be that. No, you can't be that. 25

I asked them:
Just what do you think I am?
Just a child, they said,
*And children always become
At least one of the things 30
We want them to be.*

They do not understand me.
I'll be a stable if I want, smelling of fresh hay,
I'll be a lost glade in which unicorns still play.
They do not realise I can fulfil any ambition. 35
They do not realise among them
Walks a magician.

Brian Patten

Underline the correct answers.

1 The child wanted to be the home of eagles. What was he going to be?

(a tree, an ocean, a range of mountains)

2 What does the child ultimately want to be?

(a lawyer, a beautician, a magician)

Answer these questions.

3 Find a word in the poem that rhymes with 'tree'. _____

4 Who do you think 'they' (line 7) could be?

_____

5 How does the text indicate when adults are talking?

_____

6–8 Read lines 26–31 again. What impression is given of these adults? How do you think the child might feel?

_____

_____

_____

9–10 Describe the child's character using evidence from the poem.

_____

_____

_____

Write the **plural** form of each of these **nouns**.

11 lantern _____   12 atlas _____

13 disease _____   14 chocolate _____

15 calf _____   16 athlete _____

17 fox _____   18 roof _____

Add a **verb** to complete these sentences. Each verb may be used only once.

    read   searched   ran   went   grew   felt

19 Marcus _____ for the bus.

20 Meena _____ the Internet for information on the Moon.

21 The teacher _____ the chapter to the class.

22 The flowers _____ quickly in the greenhouse.

23 Mr Robson _____ closer to the strange shape.

24 The fire-fighters _____ the force of the explosion.

Add the missing punctuation at the end of each sentence.

25 You should always wear a helmet when riding your bike ___

26 The snake slipped silently through the fallen leaves ___

27 Quick, we've got to go ___

28 Have you done your homework tonight ___

29 Hurry, before it starts to rain ___

30 What is hiding in the mess under your bed ___

31 Queen Victoria served her country for many years ___

Write a word with the same letter string and same sound as each of these words.

32 dove _____   33 borough _____

34 fought _____   35 bough _____

36 though _____   37 move _____

38 mellow _____   39 rough _____

Underline one word in each group which is not a **synonym** for the rest.

40 fast   quick   rapid   slow   speedy

41 display   hide   exhibit   demonstrate   reveal

42 guzzle   slurp   quaff   sip   gulp

43 gregarious lonesome isolated remote solitary

44 angry   sulky   cranky   furious   content

45 misleading   false   accurate   fake   untrue

46 endanger   safeguard   defend   protect   look after

Underline the **pronouns** in the following passage.

47–54 We regretted leaving our jumpers behind. It had become cold and we could have done with them for protection from the biting wind. Still we battled on against the elements. It was so important we made it before darkness fell.

Underline the silent letter in each of these words.

55 answer _____   **56** ballet _____

57 honour _____   **58** wriggle _____

59 solemn _____   **60** rhythm _____

61 island _____   **62** exhibit _____

Copy each of these **phrases** making each **noun plural**. Don't forget to add the missing apostrophe.

63–64 the two car horn _____

65–66 the five girl jumper _____

67–68 the six bird beak _____

69–70 the four dog lead _____

Add a **suffix** to each of these words.

71 resource _____

72 shape _____

73 excite _____

74 woe _____

75 remote _____

76 false _____

77 tame _____

Choose an **adverb** to fill each gap. Each **adverb** may be used only once.

cheekily   wearily   lovingly   accidentally   wistfully   angrily   tunefully

78 Alice sang _____.

79 Nina gently and _____ washed and set her Gran's hair.

80 Manjit tripped and _____ dropped the paint pot.

81 Jacob sighed _____ as he looked at the brand new sports car.

82 Sam _____ climbed into bed.

83 Tuhil yelled _____ at his dog as he chased a cat.

84 Anne _____ chuckled.

Rewrite these sentences changing them from **plural** to **singular**.

85–86 The teams played their best.

_____

87–89 The cinemas in the area were showing the latest films.

_____

90–92 The bonfires burnt for many hours.

_____

Copy the **proper nouns**, adding the missing capital letters.

93–100
february   bath rugby club   aberdeen
sydney harbour   gangster   windsor castle
contest   outcome   blue peter
ben nevis   combination   alex roberts

_____   _____

_____   _____

_____   _____

_____   _____

Now go to the Progress Chart to record your score!   Total   100

Paper 2

It was not until the first week in November that replies from the Sticklebury penpals began to trickle into class. Oliver's letter from Simon was first to arrive.

Dear Oliver Boot,

You shouldn't have said in your letter that I might never grow out of my horrible habits because my mother read that bit by mistake, and my father had to give her a whisky to stop her crying.

How are you? I am very well. I have been sent to the psi psyich pchi pei psychologist because of the worse things that were private. So they aren't quite so private any more.

I tell terrible lies. It drives them mad, but I can't help it. I also run away from school. Quite often. But then I did them both at the same time, and that was a mistake. I ran away from school after morning assembly, and my next door neighbour pounced on me while I was half in and half out of the downstairs lavatory window, sneaking back in our house. I told her the school nurse sent me home because I had headlice, which was the only thing I could think of. But that evening the next door neighbour told Mum that I mustn't come round and play with her little Peter any more till I'd been sorted out. And Mum said: Sorted Out About What? And she said: About Headlice, Of Course. And then my mum went up the wall.

I begged her not to, with real tears in my eyes, but she wrote to the school nurse anyway, demanding an explanation and an apology. But I just happened to lose the letter inside a dustbin as I walked past it. I needn't have bothered, because Mum was so angry she phoned the school anyway. And when my teacher said: Simon, Where Is The Letter From Your Mother? I just panicked and told her my mother wasn't really my mother at all because I am a long lost, secret son of the Prince, and my mum and dad just pretend I am theirs to save the Queen from unbearable embarrassment.

So then my teacher said: Oh Yes? all sarcastically. And I panicked some more and said I could prove it with my handwriting. It is this bad because I am by nature left-handed, I said, and I am forced to write with my right hand to keep up my disguise.

All Right, my teacher said. Here Is A Pen, Simon. Write With Your Left Hand. So I asked: What Shall I Write? and she said tartly: How About This Is A Shocking Pack Of Lies? So I wrote with my left hand, and it was even worse than this, if you can imagine. And when I said it was simply because I hadn't had enough practice writing with my left hand, my teacher went right up the wall.

How are you? I hope you are quite well.
    Yours sincerely,
        Simon Huggett

From A Pack of Liars by Anne Fine

Underline the correct answers.

1 (Simon's, Oliver's, Peter's) letter was first to arrive.

2 Simon thinks he was sent to the psychologist because (he tells lies, he runs away from school, he has headlice).

3 Simon (did, didn't) have headlice.

Answer these questions.

4 What is meant by the line 'replies from the Sticklebury penpals began to trickle into class' (lines 1–2)?

_____

_____

_____

5 What does Simon mean when he says 'And then my mum went up the wall' (line 16)?

_____

_____

6 Why do you think Simon highlights the fact that he had 'real' tears (line 17)?

_____

_____

_____

7–8 In lines 18–19 Simon says 'But I just happened to lose the letter inside a dustbin as I walked past it.' What did Simon really do with the letter and why do you think he phrased it the way he did?

_____

_____

_____

9–10 Do you think Simon's left-handed argument is a valid one? What does it tell us about Simon's character?

_____

_____

_____

_____

Circle the words that either are or can be **nouns**.

11–17 herd   cheese   playful   booklet
       under   Richard   antelope   fracture
       hate   secure   questioned similar

Add one of the **prefixes** to each word to make its **antonym**.

   non   im   ir   dis

18 _____responsible   19 _____existent

20 _____approve   21 _____balance

22 _____relevant   23 _____possible

24 _____charge   25 _____similar

Add the missing commas to these sentences.

26–27 Jess had to feed her cat give fresh water to the chickens take the dog for a walk and let the sheep out before school.

28–30 It was wet blustery sunny warm and windy during the Todd family walk.

31–33 Joseph spent his pocket money on a small pot of paint for his model aircraft a magazine a card for his mum's birthday a chocolate bar and a drink.

Write two **antonyms** for each of these words.

34–35 laugh   _____   _____

36–37 violent   _____   _____

38–39 small   _____   _____

Underline one **clause** (a section of a sentence with a **verb**) in each of these sentences.

40 Aimee wanted to go horse riding despite the pouring rain.
41 Nazar lost his coat at school on the coldest day of the year.
42 The snow fell heavily for many hours.
43 Dad stopped at the side of the road to answer his phone.
44 Helen ordered a cup of tea and an iced bun from the café on the high street.
45 Eleni worked hard at solving her maths problem despite her headache.

Add the **prefix** sub or tele to each of these words.

46 _____plot
47 _____standard
48 _____communications
49 _____normal
50 _____phone
51 _____merge
52 _____title
53 _____conscious

Write a more powerful **verb** for each of these verbs.

54 run _____
55 laugh _____
56 throw _____
57 swallow _____
58 wet _____
59 speak _____

Underline the **root word** for each of these words.

60 transatlantic
61 idleness
62 partnership
63 placement
64 non-toxic
65 unreal
66 dangerously
67 assessment
68 bicycle

Copy these sentences and write a **possessive pronoun** in place of the words in bold.

69–70 The apples on their side of the fence are **their apples** but those on our side are **our apples**.

_____

_____

71–72 **Your coat** is the same as **my coat**.

_____

73–74 **Kyle's bike** is bigger than **my bike**.

_____

75–76 **Jake's drink** tasted better than **Sarah's drink**.

_____

Add these **suffixes** to each word.

77 plan + ed = _____

78 admit + ing = _____

79 ballot + ed = _____

80 tax + ing = _____

81 refer + ed = _____

82 cancel + ed = _____

83 test + ed = _____

84 focus + ing = _____

85 prefer + ed = _____

86 hop + ing = _____

Add a different imperative **verb** to each of these sentences.

87 _____, there's a car coming!

88 _____, or we will be late.

89 _____, they're after us.

90 _____, in the name of the law!

91 _____ if you can't hear me at the back of the room.

92 _____ your percussion instruments.

93 _____ if you're happy!

Add *ant*, *ance*, *ent* or *ence* to complete these words.

94–95 assist _____ assist _____

96–97 toler _____ toler _____

98–99 innoc _____ innoc _____

100 obedi _____

Now go to the Progress Chart to record your score! Total

Paper 3

Preparation for a marathon takes many months but at last it is **The Big Day**.

Depending on the time of the race, make sure you eat a small meal high in carbohydrate at least three hours beforehand. You may feel too nervous to eat, but you do need to top up your liver glycogen. Glycogen can only be stored in the liver for about 12 hours and is a necessary source of energy in the latter stages of the run.

If you are staying away from home the night before the race, take a selection of the breakfast you would usually eat with you as it's best not to introduce anything different at this late stage. Don't be persuaded to alter your habits, no matter how well-meaning your host may be.

Having worked out your route to the race, set out with plenty of time, aiming to get there at least an hour before the start. Although you may find there is a very exciting atmosphere, try not to let it deflect you from your preparation. You can find yourself stopping and having chats and suddenly 20 minutes have gone by and you're not ready.

If you are with a club, they may supply transport and a safe place to store your kit, otherwise the organisers of the event will offer secure storage. Strip down to your running kit, apply the plasters, store your kit then … queue for the loo! This is a crucial activity and at some events can take up to half an hour!

Cover up before the race with an old sweat-top or black bin-bag so as to keep warm. You can discard it when you get going.

Keep a small bottle of water with you, sipping from time to time, until about 20 minutes before the start. You will be supplied with water on all races and some events will give you squash or a brand name replacement drink. Only use these if you are used to them in training, as they can upset your stomach. Some runners use energy bars and dried fruit to sustain their energy through the run; again, don't eat through the race if you're not used to it.

Set your own watch as you go over the start line, as it can be up to 10 minutes after the actual start gun, depending on the attendance at the race. That way you can monitor your own race.

Aim to run the first five miles at your predicted race speed. Being suddenly surrounded by a variety of runners can throw you off, so run your own race and don't worry about the rest.

You're off …
Enjoy the race!

From *Marathon Manual* by Cathy Shipton with Liz McColgan

Underline the correct answers.

1 You should finally eat (just before, three hours before, twelve hours before) the start of the race.

2 Why is it important to top up your glycogen levels before the race?

(it stops you feeling nervous, it tops up your energy levels, it allows you to skip breakfast)

3 Why can it sometimes take many minutes from the start of the race for the runner to actually cross the start line?

(because the runner isn't prepared, because there are many runners wanting to cross the start line, because some runners like to start the race by walking)

Answer these questions.

4 Why might the runner stay away from home the night before a race?

_____

5–6 Give two reasons why it is important to arrive approximately an hour before the race starts.

_____

_____

_____

7 Why does the author describe going to the loo as a 'crucial activity' (lines 16–17)?

_____

_____

8 What is the meaning of the word 'sustain' on line 24?

_____

9–10 Give two reasons why the use of a bin-bag or sweat-top is suggested.

_____

_____

_____

13

Add the missing *ie* or *ei* letters to complete each word correctly.

11 h_____r   12 dec_____ve   13 fr_____ght

14 v_____w   15 conc_____ve   16 y_____ld

17 n_____ghbours   18 s_____ze   19 conc_____ted

Rewrite each sentence in the first person.

20 She enjoys swimming. _____

21 They made their favourite cakes. _____

22 He loves playing football. _____

23 The teacher stopped her on the way to class.

_____

Write an **antonym** for each of these words.

24 high _____   25 cold _____

26 over _____   27 legal _____

28 difficult _____   29 mobile _____

30 bought _____   31 receive _____

32 whisper _____

Change the degree of possibility in these sentences by adding a different modal verb to each one, for example The children shall walk home from school.

33 The children _____ walk home from school.

34 The children _____ walk home from school.

35 The children _____ walk home from school.

36 The children _____ walk home from school.

37 The children _____ walk home from school.

14

Add the missing commas to these sentences.

38 Fed up because the computer continually broke down they decided to buy a new one.

39 The sunbathers lay on the beach all afternoon unaware of how burnt they were becoming.

40–41 The stranger a well-dressed man joined the party.

42 In Madagascar the inner skins of leaves are peeled and then stretched out in the tropical sun which dries and bleaches them.

43 While Henry was swimming at his local pool the lights suddenly went off.

44 When it was announced that the fancy-dress competition was about to take place we huddled together to plan our escape.

Write each of these words in its **plural** form.

45 punch _____ **46** bus _____

47 sausage _____ **48** convoy _____

49 dress _____ **50** waltz _____

51 tariff _____ **52** thief _____

Underline the **nouns** in this poem.

53–60 Daisy, Daisy,
Give me your answer do,
I'm half crazy
All for the love of you;
It won't be a stylish marriage,

For I can't afford a carriage –
But you'll look sweet
Upon the seat
Of a bicycle made for two!

Anon.

Rewrite these sentences and add the missing inverted commas.

61–64 What do we do now? grumbled Jay through gritted teeth. They're bound to sabotage our camp.

They can't do anything until it gets dark, consoled Mimi. We'll just have to make sure we stay up all through the night.

_____
_____
_____
_____

65–68 I'm frozen, complained Jay. It really is cold and dark, he sighed. Maybe they aren't going to come back tonight.

Mimi considered Jay's comment. But maybe they will! she replied.

_____

_____

_____

_____

Write one word for each **definition**. Each word begins with '*g*'.

69 A hard, transparent substance that is easily broken. _____

70 A Roman man who was forced to fight for public amusement. _____

71 A movement that conveys a meaning. _____

72 A sphere showing the map of the world. _____

73 A valuable, yellow metal. _____

74 A small, flying insect that can bite people. _____

75 A slope. _____

76 Another name for rubbish. _____

Underline the correct **homophone** in each bracket.

77–78 The (boy, buoy) untied his boat from the (boy, buoy).

79–80 The (fair, fare) for a ride at the (fair, fare) was £3.00.

81–82 Jason (new, knew) his (new, knew) jeans would fit perfectly.

83–84 'Are you (sure/shore) we can see the (sure/shore) from here?' asked the children.

85–86 The (ewe, yew) died after eating the (ewe, yew), a very poisonous plant.

Underline the sentences with **indirect speech** and write them again as direct speech.

87–94 Kate's dad called to her to hurry up.

'What's the time?' the teacher asked.

'Let's go to the playground,' pleaded the twins.

Sarah explained to Pete she was going on holiday soon.

The Singh family yelled to the passing boat that they needed help.

'Quick! The match starts in 10 minutes,' called Joel.

Mum asked her friend if she thought it might rain today.

'Have you found a snail yet?' queried Aimee.

_____

_____

_____

_____

Write the **diminutive** for each of these.

95 pig   _____   96 book   _____

97 duck   _____   98 hill   _____

99 owl   _____   100 statue _____

Now go to the Progress Chart to record your score!   Total

Paper 4

'This is Lord Fauntleroy, Mrs Mellon,' he said. 'Lord Fauntleroy, this is Mrs Mellon, who is the housekeeper.'

   Cedric gave her his hand, his eyes lighting up.

   'Was it you who sent the cat?' he said. 'I'm much obliged to you ma'am.'

   Mrs Mellon's handsome old face looked as pleased as the face of the lodge-keeper's wife had done.

   'I should know his lordship anywhere,' she said to Mr Havisham. 'He has the Captain's face and way. It's a great day, this, sir.'

   Cedric wondered why it was a great day. He looked at Mrs Mellon curiously. It seemed to him for a moment as if there were tears in her eyes, and yet it was evident she was not unhappy. She smiled down at him.

   'The cat left two beautiful kittens here,' she said. 'They shall be sent up to your lordship's nursery.'

   Mr Havisham said a few words to her in a low voice.

   'In the library, sir,' Mrs Mellon replied. 'His lordship is to be taken there alone.'

   A few minutes later the very tall footman in livery, who had escorted Cedric to the library door, opened it and announced: 'Lord Fauntleroy, my lord,' in quite a majestic tone. If he was only a footman, he felt it was rather a grand occasion when the heir came home to his own land and possessions, and was ushered into the presence of the old Earl, whose place and title he was to take.

17

Cedric crossed the threshold into the room. It was a very large and splendid room, with massive carven furniture in it, and shelves upon shelves of books … For a moment Cedric thought there was nobody in the room, but soon he saw that by the fire burning on the wide hearth there was a large easy chair, and that in that chair someone was sitting – someone who did not at first turn to look at him. 25

But he had attracted attention in one quarter at least. On the floor, by the armchair, lay a dog, a huge tawny mastiff with body and limbs almost as big as a lion's; and this great creature rose majestically and slowly, and marched towards the little fellow with a heavy step.

Then the person in the chair spoke. 'Dougal,' he called, 'come back, sir.' … 30

Cedric put his hand on the big dog's collar in the most natural way in the world, and they strayed forward together, Dougal sniffing as he went.

And then the Earl looked up …

… Cedric looked at him just as he had looked at the woman at the lodge and at the housekeeper, and came quite close to him. 35

'Are you the Earl?' he said. 'I'm your grandson, you know, that Mr Havisham brought. I'm Lord Fauntleroy.'

He held out his hand because he thought it must be the polite and proper thing to do even with earls. 'I hope you are very well,' he continued, with the utmost friendliness. 'I'm very glad to see you.' 40

The Earl shook hands with him, with a curious gleam in his eyes; just at first he was so astonished that he scarcely knew what to say. He stared at the picturesque little apparition from under his shaggy brows, and took it all in from head to foot.

'Glad to see me, are you?' he said.

From *Little Lord Fauntleroy* by Frances Hodgson Burnett

Underline the correct answers.

1 Lord Fauntleroy's first name is (Mr Havisham, Dougal, **Cedric**).

2 Mrs Mellon had tears in her eyes because she (had dust in them, was sad, was happy).

3 On line 43 the Earl is described as having 'shaggy brows'. They are a description of his (fringe, **eyebrows**, an item of clothing).

Answer these questions.

4 What piece of evidence in the passage suggests that Mrs Mellon had been housekeeper for the Earl for many years?

5 Why was it a 'great day' (line 8)?

6 Explain why when speaking to Mrs Mellon, Mr Havisham did so 'in a low voice' (line 14).

_____

_____

7 Explain in your own words what is meant by the sentence 'But he had attracted attention in one quarter at least' (line 26).

_____

_____

8–9 Find two pieces of evidence that suggest this passage was written many years ago.

_____

_____

_____

10 Why do you think the Earl 'scarcely knew what to say' (line 42) on meeting Little Lord Fauntleroy?

_____

_____

Underline the correct form of the **verb** to complete each sentence.

11 The dogs race/races after the ball.

12 Ben stir/stirs the cake mixture.

13 The chick learns to scratch/scratches the earth.

14 The Head Teacher sing/sings loudly and clearly during assembly.

15 The rain pour/pours down on the washing hung on the line.

16 Rashid peel/peels a banana.

17 The duck feed/feeds greedily on the bread.

Extend each of these words into a different **compound word**.

18 table_____   19 table_____

20 any_____   21 any_____

22 snow_____   23 snow_____

24 hand_____   25 hand_____

26 some_____   27 some_____

Add a different **adjective** in each gap to complete the sentences.

28 All the children liked the _____ classroom.

29 The _____ spoon was used for cake-making.

30 George didn't like his _____ teacher.

31 The _____ chickens scratched in the vegetable garden.

32 Eva's _____ computer made researching her homework much easier.

33 The Asser family excitedly headed towards the _____ circus.

Write a word to match each clue. Each word ends in a vowel.

34 A small wind instrument _____

35 A mountain with a crater _____

36 A folding frame covered with fabric which opens to give protection _____

37 A liquid for washing hair _____

38 Tiny pieces of coloured paper, often thrown over newlyweds _____

39 A flat round of dough covered with a savoury mixture _____

40–45 Write an account of a car accident. Include an adverbial of time, an adverbial of place, two question marks and two exclamation marks.

_____

_____

_____

_____

_____

_____

With a line, match the words with the same key spelling patterns.

46	experience	balance
47	thorough	agent
48	performance	optician
49	plumber	borough
50	entrant	licence
51	present	instant
52	electrician	numbness

Write whether each of these sentences refers to something happening in the **past**, **present** or **future**.

53 I walked home. _____

54 I am going to buy lunch. _____

55 I wrote an exciting story. _____

56 I am sipping my soup carefully. _____

57 I have made some cakes. _____

58 I will tidy my bedroom. _____

59 I am typing at my computer. _____

Write each of these words adding the **suffix** *ful* correctly.

60 thought _____ 61 awe _____

62 pity _____ 63 deceit _____

64 shame _____ 65 mercy _____

66 hope _____ 67 dread _____

Complete each sentence by adding a different **conjunction**.

68 I still went swimming _____ I had a bad cold.

69 Laurel chose to go to Horseworld for her birthday treat _____ she loves horses.

70 Mum bought me some new trainers _____ I could run faster!

71 Niall wanted to go out on his bike _____ it was raining.

72 Wusai missed a day off school _____ so did Gina.

73 Jacob has been able to use a knife and fork _____ he was three.

74 Dan's new puppy couldn't go for a walk _____ he had all his injections.

75 We left the swimming pool _____ it was closing.

Write which animal these **onomatopoeic** words remind you of.

76 roar _____ 77 baa _____

78 grunt _____ 79 gobble _____

80 mew _____ 81 cluck _____

82 woof _____

Underline the **pronouns** in the sentences.

83–84 We must buy him a packet as well.

85–87 Where is mine? Have you got it?

88–89 His is longer than yours.

90 Why are theirs the same?

91–92 I wonder what they are doing.

22

Rewrite these words adding the **suffix** *able* or *ible* to each one.

93 adore _____   94 notice _____

95 collapse _____   96 access _____

97 desire _____   98 reverse _____

99 sense _____   100 move _____

Now go to the Progress Chart to record your score!   Total   100

Paper 5

Water in Our World

Three-quarters of Earth's surface is covered by water and
nearly all of it is contained in the oceans and seas.
The rest, a very small amount, is in the air or froze long ago
to form polar ice caps. Most of the water we use comes from
rivers and lakes, or water that has seeped through rocks and collected underground.   5

- The movement of water between the land, the sea and the air is called the water
  cycle. As the Sun heats the water in the oceans, rivers, lakes and plants, some of
  the water evaporates, which means that it changes into water vapour (a gas) and
  rises into the air. High in the sky, the water vapour cools and changes back into tiny
  drops of liquid water. This process is called condensation. The water drops   10
  gather together to make clouds and eventually fall as rain, hail or snow. The cycle
  then starts all over again. As a result of this recycling, the amount of water on Earth
  always remains the same.
- About 97 per cent of all water is the salty water of the oceans and seas. The sea is
  salty because salts are either washed off the land by rivers or escape from   15
  cracks in the ocean floor. Other salts come from undersea volcanoes.
- Water makes up the greatest part of the bodies of plants and animals and is vital
  for all life. Did you know that your body is made up of more than 70 per cent water?
  You need to take in about two litres of water a day, and much more when it is hot or
  you are working hard. Aquatic animals live surrounded by water, but those that   20
  live on land have to find water or get all that they need from their food.
- Sea water has no colour, but appears blue or green because both blue and
  green light from the Sun reach deeper below the surface of the water than
  other colours. The sea also reflects the colour of the sky and changes in the
  weather.   25

From *Questions and Answers: Oceans and Rivers* by Barbara Taylor

Underline the correct answers.

1 What is the Earth's surface mainly covered in?

(land, water, land and water equally)

2 What percentage of water on Earth is salty?

(3%, 70%, 97%)

3 What colour is sea water?

(blue, green, clear)

Answer these questions.

4 Why is condensation described as a 'recycling' process (line 12)?

_____

_____

_____

_____

5 What does the word 'reflects' mean (line 24)?

_____

_____

6–7 Give two reasons why the sea is salty.

_____

_____

_____

_____

8–9 Read this sentence: *If people don't get enough water from eating and drinking they may become dehydrated*. In which bullet point would this sentence best fit and why?

_____

_____

10 Look again at the third bullet point. Write a subheading in the form of a question for this paragraph.

_____

_____

Circle the **preposition** (a word that relates other words to each other) in each of these sentences.

11 Gran slept for hours in the armchair.

12 Jay jumped behind the leather sofa.

13 Caroline walked carefully among the bluebells.

14 Yousef climbed up the cliff wall.

15 The twins looked through the letterbox to see if anyone was home.

16 The electrician slipped down the ladder and broke his leg.

17–18 Mum placed the drinks on the tray before carrying them up the stairs.

Write the short form often used for each of these words.

19 aeroplane _____

20 handkerchief _____

21 head-teacher _____

22 newspaper _____

23 champion _____

24 examination _____

Add *cial* or *tial* to complete these words.

25 commer _____

26 par _____

27 confiden _____

28 artifi _____

29 ini _____

30 spe _____

31 finan _____

Write a **synonym** for each of the words in bold.

32 The captured soldiers were **interrogated**. _____

33 Mum complained about the **racket** my music made. _____

34 I was surprised that such a famous person looked so **ordinary**.

_____

35 Dave was given the **option** to go ice-skating or to the cinema.

_____

36 The Captain **reviewed** his troops. _____

37 The rope around their wrists was **taut**. _____

38 That's **wonderful** news! _____

Rewrite these sentences, adding the missing punctuation.

39–42 What time does the party start Helen called

_____

_____

43–49 We must concentrate said David If we don't get this work done we'll have to miss our playtime

_____

_____

Match to each of these words a word with the same letter string but a different sound.

stove   height   barn   head   glove   plead

50 weight _____   51 earn _____

52 love   _____   53 bead _____

54 drove   _____   55 dead _____

Rewrite these sentences without the double negatives.

56 Jake hasn't walked no half-marathon.

_____

57 There wasn't no milk left by the milkman.

_____

58 Cath hasn't no drink for her lunch.

_____

59 Dad's not never going there again.

_____

60 There aren't no red squirrels here.

_____

61 I don't not have enough money to buy that.

_____

Write a **homophone** for each of these words.

62 site _____ **63** boarder _____

64 horse _____ **65** stationary _____

66 flower _____ **67** shore _____

68 wave _____ **69** sundae _____

Add a powerful **verb** in the gaps to make each sentence interesting.

70–71 The dog _____ towards the sea and _____ into it.

72–73 The plane _____ and the passengers _____.

74–75 '_____ or we'll never win the relay race!' _____ the team.

76–77 The children _____ through the snow until they could _____ the shining lights.

78–79 As the queen _____ the crowd _____.

Put these counties in **alphabetical order**.

Northumberland   Somerset   Suffolk   Norfolk
South Glamorgan   Nottinghamshire   Strathclyde

80 (1) _____   **81** (2) _____

82 (3) _____   **83** (4) _____

84 (5) _____   **85** (6) _____

86 (7) _____

Underline the **conjunctions** (a word or words that join clauses or sentences) in each sentence.

87 Ella had to sit down for tea even though her favourite programme was on.

88 Daniel needed his boots but he couldn't find them.

89 The runner stopped the race after he hurt his ankle.

90 Veejay handed in his homework although it was past the deadline.

91 The kittens drank their milk and chased the ball before settling down for the night.

92 It was time for Jane to go home though she wanted to stay longer.

Circle the words which have a soft 'g'.

93–100 knowledge   gaggle   garage   imagine   gourd   refugee   generous
governor   dungeon   gradient   gigantic   grime   message   wrong   frog

Now go to the Progress Chart to record your score!   Total   100

Paper 6

When the end of the war did come, it came swiftly, almost unexpectedly it seemed to the men around me. There was little joy, little celebration of victory, only a sense of profound relief that at last it was finished and done with. Albert left the happy cluster of men gathered together in the yard that cold November morning and strolled over to talk to me. 'Five minutes time and it'll be finished, Joey, all over. Jerry's had about enough of it, and so have we. No one really wants to go on any more. At eleven o'clock the guns will stop and then that will be that. Only wish that David could have been here to see it.'

Since David's death Albert had not been himself. I had not once seen him smile or joke, and he often fell into prolonged brooding silences when he was with me. There was no more singing, no more whistling. I tried all that I could to comfort him, resting my head on his shoulder and nickering gently to him, but he seemed quite inconsolable. Even the news that the war was finally ending brought no light back to his eyes. The bell in the clock tower over the gateway rang out eleven times, and the men shook each other solemnly by the hand or clapped each other on the back before returning to the stables.

The fruits of victory were to prove bitter indeed for me, but to begin with the end of the war changed little. The Veterinary Hospital operated as it always had done, and the flow of sick and injured horses seemed rather to increase than to diminish. From the yard gate we saw the unending columns of fighting men marching jauntily back to the railway stations, and we looked on as the tanks and guns and wagons rolled by on their way home. But we were left where we were. Like the other men, Albert was becoming impatient. Like them he wanted only to get home as quickly as possible.

Morning parade took place as usual every morning in the centre of the cobbled yard, followed by Major Martin's inspection of the horses and stables. But one dreary, drizzling morning, with the wet cobbles shining grey in the early morning light, Major Martin did not inspect the stables as usual. Sergeant 'Thunder' stood the men at ease and Major Martin announced the re-embarkation plans for the unit. He was finishing his short speech: 'So we shall be at Victoria Station by six o'clock on Saturday evening – with any luck. Chances are you'll be home by Christmas.'

'Permission to speak, sir?' Sergeant 'Thunder' ventured.

'Carry on, Sergeant.'

'It's about the 'orses, sir,' Sergeant 'Thunder' said. 'I think the men would like to know what's going to 'appen with the 'orses. Will they be with us on the same ship, sir? Or will they be coming along later?'

Major Martin shifted his feet and looked down at his boots. He spoke softly as he did not want to be heard. 'No, Sergeant,' he said. 'I'm afraid the horses won't be coming with us at all.'

From *War Horse* by Michael Morpurgo

Underline the correct answers.

   1 In which month did the war end?

      (October, November, December)

2 Who is Joey?

(a soldier friend of Albert's, a wounded soldier, a horse)

Answer these questions.

3 Why had Albert 'not been himself' (line 9)?

_____

4 What was the significance of the bell at the gateway ringing out eleven times?

_____

_____

5 Write another word the author could have used instead of 'nickering' (line 12).

_____

6–7 Give the meaning of the following words as they are used in the passage:

profound (line 3) _____

jauntily (line 20) _____

8–9 Using evidence from the passage, describe how you think war has affected Albert.

_____

_____

_____

_____

10 In lines 37–38 the sergeant 'spoke softly as he did not want to be heard'. Why?

_____

_____

_____

Write the **collective noun** for each of these living creatures.

11 elephants _____ **12** sheep _____

13 kittens _____ **14** ants _____

15 fish _____ **16** lions _____

17 bees _____ **18** seagulls _____

Write six sentences, each with a relative clause beginning with the following words or an omitted pronoun.

19 who _____

20 which _____

21 that _____

22 whose _____

23 whom _____

24 omitted pronoun _____

Add *ory*, *ery* or *ary* to each of these words.

25 Febru_____   26 diction_____   27 hist_____

28 myst_____   29 ordin_____   30 secret_____

31 jewell_____   32 necess_____   33 mem_____

Add the missing apostrophe or apostrophes to each sentence.

34 Dont go over there!

35 We couldve gone to the beach.

36 Theyll be home soon.

37–38 Its time to go to ballet, isnt it?

39 I shant eat my tea!

40 Well buy some sweets tomorrow.

31

Complete each of these expressions using the words below.

   bush   cart   apple   ghost   head   rat   heart

41 Don't give up the _____.

42 To smell a _____.

43 To hang your _____ in shame.

44 To put the _____ before the horse.

45 Absence makes the _____ grow fonder.

46 Don't beat about the _____.

47 An _____ a day keeps the doctor away.

Rewrite these book titles, adding the missing capital letters.

48–50 classic children's stories

_____

51–54 the little book of facts

_____

55–58 keeping ponies season by season

_____

Circle the word which is …

59 a **verb**	bus	happily	bounce	it
60 a **pronoun**	they	ran	through	rain
61 a **noun**	tree	but	pretty	before
62 an **adverb**	gate	new	kicked	greedily
63 a **preposition**	under	marmalade	we	you
64 an **adjective**	jacket	lank	love	swarm
65 a **conjunction**	hidden	giant	cold	although

Some questions will be answered in the children's own words. Answers to these questions are given in *italics*. Any answers that seem to be in line with these should be marked correct.

Paper 1 (pages 2–6)

1 **a range of mountains** (lines 21 and 23)
2 **a magician** (line 37)
3 Acceptable answers could include any of the following: me, be, MC, we, TV.
4 **adults, such as parents or teachers** In lines 28–31 the poet is told that he is 'Just a child' and that 'children become at least one of the things we want them to be'. This suggests he is talking to someone older than himself.
5 *The words are written in italics.*
6–8 *The adults are controlling; they haven't really listened to the child; the child might be feeling put down and dismissed.*
9–10 *The child is confident and believes in him or herself. For example, even after being told by the parents that he or she can't be lots of things, the child continues to believe that he or she can be. This is shown when the child says, 'They do not realise I can fulfil any ambition'.*
11–18 In most cases the letter 's' just needs to be added, or if the word ends in 's', 'ss', 'ff', 'sh', 'ch', 'x' or 'z' then 'es' is added. If a word ends in a single letter 'f' then the 'f' is removed and 'ves' is added. However, there are exceptions to this rule (for example 'beliefs' and 'roofs') and these words need to be learned separately.
11 **lanterns** The letter 's' just needs to be added.
12 **atlases** As the word ends in 's', 'es' needs to be added.
13 **diseases** Refer to question 11.
14 **chocolates** Refer to question 11.
15 **calves** The 'f' needs to be removed and 'ves' is added.
16 **athletes** Refer to question 11.
17 **foxes** As the word ends in 'x', 'es' needs to be added.
18 **roofs** Unlike other words that end in 'f', 'roof' is an exception to the rule and 's' just needs to be added.
19 Marcus **ran** for the bus.
20 Meena **searched** the Internet for information on the Moon.
21 The teacher **read** the chapter to the class.
22 The flowers **grew** quickly in the greenhouse.
23 Mr Robinson **went** closer to the strange shape.
24 The fire-fighters **felt** the force of the explosion.

25–31 A full stop is needed at the end of a simple statement. A question mark is needed at the end of a question. An exclamation mark is needed at the end of a sentence to show that something is surprising, being shouted or being said with strong emotion.
25 You should always wear a helmet when riding your bike.
26 The snake slipped silently through the fallen leaves.
27 Quick, we've got to go!
28 Have you done your homework tonight?
29 Hurry, before it starts to rain!
30 What is hiding in the mess under your bed?
31 Queen Victoria served her country for many years.
32–39 A letter string is a small group of letters that appears in many words. In this case, the letter strings are 'ove', 'ough', 'ought', and 'ellow'. Some letter strings can be pronounced in more than one way and the answer needs to rhyme with each given word. Possible answers:
32 *glove*
33 *thorough*
34 *brought*
35 *plough*
36 *dough*
37 *prove*
38 *bellow*
39 *tough*
40–46 A synonym is a word that has the same, or similar, meaning to another word. For example, 'gigantic' is a synonym of 'large'.
40 **slow**
41 **hide**
42 **sip**
43 **gregarious**
44 **content**
45 **accurate**
46 **endanger**
47–54 A pronoun is a word that replaces a noun in a sentence to avoid repetition. Examples of pronouns are: I, she, they, it, and we.
We regretted leaving our jumpers behind. **It** had become cold and **we** could have done with **them** for protection from the biting wind. Still **we** battled on against the elements. **It** was so important **we** made **it** before darkness fell.
55 ans**w**er
56 balle**t**
57 **h**onour
58 **w**riggle
59 solem**n**
60 r**h**ythm

ANSWERS

61 i**s**land
62 ex**h**ibit
63–70 A noun is a person, place or thing. To show that something belongs to more than one, add an 's' followed by an apostrophe (s').
63–64 **the two cars' horns**
65–66 **the five girls' jumpers**
67–68 **the six birds' beaks**
69–70 **the four dogs' leads**
71–77 A suffix is a group of letters that are added to the end of a word. Examples of suffixes are 'ment', 'tion', 'sion' or 'ful'. Possible answers:
71 *resourceful*
72 *shapeless*
73 *excitement*
74 *woeful*
75 *remoteness*
76 *falsehood*
77 *tameness*
78 Alice sang **tunefully**.
79 Nina gently and **lovingly** washed and set her Gran's hair.
80 Manjit tripped and **accidentally** dropped the paint pot.
81 Jacob sighed **wistfully** as he looked at the brand new sports car.
82 Sam **wearily** climbed into bed.
83 Tuhil yelled **angrily** at his dog as he chased a cat.
84 Anne **cheekily** chuckled.
85–86 To change the sentences from plural to singular, the 's' will need to be removed from the noun. Make sure pronouns and verbs (such as 'was' or 'were') are also changed correctly.
85–86 The **team** played **its** best.
87–89 The **cinema** in the area **was** showing the latest **film**.
90–92 The **bonfire** burnt for **an hour**.
93–100 A proper noun is the name of a person, place or thing. It always has a capital letter.
February, Bath Rugby Club, Aberdeen, Sydney Harbour, Windsor Castle, Blue Peter, Ben Nevis, Alex Roberts

Paper 2 (pages 7–11)

1 **Oliver's** The introductory text tells us that Oliver's letter was the first to arrive.
2 **he tells lies** (lines 7–9)
3 **didn't** (lines 12–14)
4 *Responses from the penpals began to arrive, a few at a time, in class.*
5 *His mother became angry/upset.*
6 *To emphasise the fact that he was really upset and not just pretending.*
7–8 *Simon actually threw the letter in the dustbin. He said that he accidentally lost it because he didn't want to admit that he threw it away.*
9–10 *Simon's argument is not valid and is obviously made up to support the outrageous lie he has told. The lie does show, however, that Simon has a good imagination.*
11–17 The following are different types of nouns: a common noun is a person, place or thing; a proper noun is the name of a person, place or thing; a collective noun is a word describing a group; and an abstract noun is a thought, feeling or idea. Therefore, the following words are nouns:
herd, cheese, booklet, Richard, antelope, fracture, hate
18–25 A prefix is a small group of letters added to the beginning of a word which adjusts the meaning. When a prefix is added, the spelling of the original word does not need to change. An antonym is a word that has the opposite meaning. Some prefixes need a hyphen between it and the root word.
18 **irresponsible**
19 **non-existent**
20 **disapprove**
21 **imbalance**
22 **irrelevant**
23 **impossible**
24 **discharge**
25 **dissimilar**
26–33 Commas are used to separate words or phrases in a list. No comma is needed between the last two items in the list, only the word 'and'. For example: *I went to the shop to buy some bread, eggs, butter and milk*; or *I packed some toothpaste, an extra blanket and some paperback books.*
26–27 Jess had to feed her cat, give fresh water to the chickens, take the dog for a walk and let the sheep out before school.
28–30 It was wet, blustery, sunny, warm and windy during the Todd family walk.
31–33 Joseph spent his pocket money on a small pot of paint for his model aircraft, a magazine, a card for his mum's birthday, a chocolate bar and a drink.
34–39 Refer to Q18–25 on antonyms. Here are some possible answers.
34–35 *cry, snivel, weep*
36–37 *calm, friendly, gentle*
38–39 *huge, gigantic, massive*

A2

72 **easily** As the root word 'easy' ends with a consonant followed by 'y', the 'y' is replaced with 'i' and 'ly' is added.
73 **employed** As the root word 'employ' ends in a vowel followed by 'y', the suffix 'ed' just needs to be added.
74 **spying** This is an exception to the rule as the root word is a three-letter word ending in 'y'. The suffix 'ing' just needs to be added.
75 **buyer** As the root word 'buy' ends in a vowel followed by 'y', the suffix 'er' just needs to be added.
76 **beautiful** As the root word 'beauty' ends with a consonant followed by 'y', the 'y' is replaced with 'i' and 'ful' is added.
77 **merriment** As the root word 'merry' ends with a consonant followed by 'y', the 'y' is replaced with 'i' and 'ment' is added.
78 **future** The words 'will be' show us the action will be in the future.
79 **past** The word 'opened' shows us the action has happened in the past.
80 **present** The words 'You're eating' show us the action is happening now.
81 **present** The words 'is leaving' show us the action is happening now.
82 **future** The words 'will soak' show us the action will be in the future.
83 **present** The word 'is' shows us the action is happening now.
84 **past** The word 'stopped' shows us the action has happened in the past.
85 **past** The word 'blew' shows us the action has happened in the past.

86–91

France	Germany	Italy
croissant	schnitzel	studio
boutique	kindergarten	ravioli

92–97 Refer to the following: Paper 1 Q63–70 on nouns; Paper 2 Q40–45 on verbs; and Paper 1 Q71–77 on suffixes.
92 **frighten**
93 **signify**
94 **solidify**
95 **fossilise**
96 **glorify**
97 **apologise**
98 He **has** returned the library book in time so won't receive a fine.
99 Rachel **did** the dishes after lunch.
100 They **are** expected to begin the competition at noon.

Paper 12 (pages 63–67)

1 **between and a lake and a forest** (line 1, 2, and 5)
2 **old** (line 8)
3 **fretful** (line 13)
4–6 **Linden wood (limewood); moss and rushes; reindeer sinews** (lines 10–12)
7–8 *Native American. The poem uses the word 'wigwam' which is a Native American cone-shaped dwelling.*
9–10 *It was important so he could grow up watching out for dangers but also to understand the ways of his people.*
11 r**h**inoceros
12 buffe**t**
13 scra**t**ch
14 ras**p**berry
15 bisc**u**it
16 **w**ristwatch
17 **h**eiress
18 s**w**ord
19–24 A parenthesis is a word or phrase that has been inserted into a sentence. If it is removed, the sentence will still make sense without it. The parenthesis will have either commas, brackets or dashes directly before and after it.
25–40 Refer to Paper 2 Q11–17 on nouns.

Proper nouns	Abstract nouns	Common nouns	Collective nouns
Bath Rugby Club	jealousy	desk	colony
Iraq	dislike	holiday	gaggle
Keswick	beauty	microscope	flock
Charlie	love	puppy	bunch

41–45 Refer to Paper 4 Q76–82 on onomatopoeia.
41 *splash, splat*
42 *vroom*
43 *squelch*
44 *crackle*
45 *crash, bang*
46–53 Refer to Paper 6 Q34–40 on contractions.
46 **they've**
47 **there'll**
48 **wouldn't**
49 **shan't**
50 **it's**
51 **I'll**
52 **could've**
53 **doesn't**
54 Monty the dog slept soundly (*as, because*) he was exhausted after his walk.

55 Tariq received his swimming certificate (as, after, **because**) he swam 30 lengths of the pool.
56 Sophie was very excited (as, **because**, when) she was having a sleepover at Helen's house.
57 Dan dropped the books he was holding (after, as, because, **when**) Meena gave him a fright.

58–65 Refer to Paper 2 Q18–25 on prefixes.
58 **impatient**
59 **unpleasant**
60 **illiterate**
61 **uninterested**
62 **illegible**
63 **unreliable**
64 **impossible**
65 **illogical**

66–86 'What are we going to do?' I wailed. 'We are really going to be in trouble this time.'
'Only if they catch us,' replied Finn.
'But they are bound to,' I mumbled.

87–94 Refer to the following: Paper 4 Q28–33 on adjectives; Paper 1 Q47–54 on pronouns; Paper 5 Q11–18 on prepositions; and Paper 3 Q38–44 on conjunctions. Here are some possible answers.

87–88 *cloudy, heavy*
89–90 *you, she*
91–92 *behind, over*
93–94 *as, because*

95–100 Refer to Paper 2 Q60–68 on root words.
95 **thought** The suffixes 'less' and 'ness' have been added.
96 **assist** The suffix 'ance' has been added.
97 **possess** The suffix 'ion' has been added.
98 **assemble** The 'e' has been replaced with the suffix 'y'.
99 **help** The prefix 'un' and the suffix 'ful' have been added.
100 **compute** As the root word already ends in 'e', then 'r' is added to make the 'er' suffix and form the word 'computer'.

40–45 A clause is a group of words. Some clauses can be complete sentences. Every clause needs a verb which is an 'action word'. Examples of verbs are: was walking, sat, typed, etc.
- 40 **Aimee wanted to go horse riding** despite the pouring rain.
- 41 **Nazar lost his coat** at school on the coldest day of the year.
- 42 **The snow fell heavily** for many hours.
- 43 **Dad stopped at the side of the road** to answer his phone.
- 44 **Helen ordered a cup of tea and an iced bun** from the café on the high street.
- 45 **Eleni worked hard at solving her maths problem** despite her headache.

46–53 Refer to Q18–25 on prefixes.
- 46 **sub**plot
- 47 **sub**standard
- 48 **tele**communications
- 49 **sub**normal
- 50 **tele**phone
- 51 **sub**merge
- 52 **sub**title
- 53 **sub**conscious

54–59 A more powerful verb will be a synonym, a word that has the same meaning as the words shown, but is more specific. For example, a more powerful verb than *talk* could be *whisper* or *chat*. Here are some possible answers:
- 54 *sprint, race*
- 55 *guffaw, chuckle, giggle*
- 56 *fling*
- 57 *gulp*
- 58 *soak, drench*
- 59 *yell, scream*

60–68 A root word is the most basic form of a word which is able to have a prefix or suffix added to it. For example, the root word 'appear' can have the prefix 'dis' added to form the word 'disappear' or the suffix 'ance' added to it to form the word 'appearance'.
- 60 trans**atlantic** The prefix 'trans' has been added.
- 61 idle**ness** The suffix 'ness' has been added.
- 62 part**ner**ship or partner**ship** The suffixes 'ner' and 'ship' have been added. (These are not common suffixes and children might not know them.)
- 63 place**ment** The suffix 'ment' has been added.
- 64 non-**toxic** The prefix 'non' has been added. The 'non' prefix is usually followed by a hyphen.
- 65 **un**real The prefix 'un' has been added.
- 66 danger**ously** or **danger**ously The suffixes 'ous' and 'ly' have been added.
- 67 assess**ment** The suffix 'ment' has been added.
- 68 **bi**cycle The prefix 'bi' has been added.

69–76 A possessive pronoun is a pronoun that shows ownership. Examples of possessive pronouns are: mine, his, theirs, yours, ours, etc.
- 69–70 The apples on their side of the fence are **theirs** but those on our side are **ours**.
- 71–72 **Yours** is the same as **mine**.
- 73–74 **His** is bigger than **mine**.
- 75–76 **His** tasted better than **hers**.

77–86 Usually, the last letter is doubled or left single according to the vowel sound. However, many of the following spellings are an exception to this rule and these spellings need to be learned individually.
- 77 **planned** The last letter is doubled as 'plan' has a short vowel sound.
- 78 **admitting** The last letter is doubled as the last syllable has a short vowel sound.
- 79 **balloted** This is an exception to the rule of adding a suffix to a word ending in a short vowel sound and the suffix 'ed' just needs to be added.
- 80 **taxing**
- 81 **referred** This is an exception to the rule of adding a suffix to a word ending in a long vowel sound. The last letter is doubled and 'ed' is added.
- 82 **cancelled**
- 83 **tested**
- 84 **focussing** or **focusing**
- 85 **preferred**
- 86 **hopping**

87–93 An imperative verb is a word that tells someone to do something. Examples are: take, wait, put or go. Possible answers:
- 87 *Stop*
- 88 *Hurry*
- 89 *Run*
- 90 *Halt*
- 91 *Shout*
- 92 *Rattle*
- 93 *Smile*

94-100 There are many rules for adding these suffixes but the only rule that applies here is that if the root word ends in the letters 'ate', then the suffixes 'ant' or 'ance' are added. Words that end in 'ant' or 'ance' are much more common than words ending in 'ent' or 'ence', but many of these spellings need to be learned individually.
- 94–95 **ant, ance** assistant, assistance
- 96–97 **ant, ance** tolerant, tolerance (The root would, 'tolerate' ends in the suffix 'ate', so 'ant' and 'ance' are added.)
- 98–99 **ent, ence** innocent, innocence
- 100 **ent, ence** obedient or obedience

Paper 3 (pages 12–17)

1. **three hours before** (lines 2–3)
2. **it tops up your energy levels** (lines 4–5)
3. **because there are many runners wanting to cross the start line** (lines 25–26)
4. *because the race is a distance from the runner's own home*
5–6. *to allow plenty of preparation time; to allow for delays getting to the race*
7. *It isn't easy to stop part way through a race to go to the toilet.*
8. *to keep up one's energy levels*
9–10. *to keep warm; they are of no value so can be thrown away once taken off*
11–19. The letters 'ei' are usually added after the letter 'c' in a word and 'ie' is used after all other letters. However, there are exceptions to this rule (such as seize, neither, foreign, etc) and these spellings need to be learnt separately.
11. heir
12. deceive
13. freight
14. view
15. conceive
16. yield
17. neighbours
18. seize
19. conceited
20. I enjoy swimming.
21. I made my favourite cakes.
22. I love playing football.
23. **The teacher stopped me on the way to class/I stopped her on the way to class.**
24–32. Refer to Paper 2 Q18–25 on antonyms. Possible answers.
24. *low*
25. *hot*
26. *under*
27. *illegal*
28. *easy*
29. *stationary, still, immobile*
30. *sold*
31. *give*
32. *shout*
33–37. Modal verbs are words that tell us how likely something is going to happen. Examples of modal verbs are: *will, might, should, must, can, may.* Child's answer should include a different modal verb for each question.
38–44. Commas are used to separate clauses. A main clause is a sentence that can stand on its own (such as '*He is walking to school.*'). A subordinate clause begins with a conjunction and cannot be a sentence on its own (such as '*as the bus was late*'). Other examples of conjunctions are: if, while, although, etc. Commas also surround additional information (an embedded clause) within a sentence. For instance, in questions 40–41, '*a well-dressed man*' is additional information – the sentence will still make sense without these words – therefore a comma needs to go before and after this phrase. If an adverbial starts the sentence then a comma is needed after that adverbial (such as 'At midnight, the fox crept across the lawn).
38. Fed up because the computer continually broke down, they decided to buy a new one.
39. The sunbathers lay on the beach all afternoon, unaware of how burnt they were becoming.
40–41. The stranger, a well-dressed man, joined the party.
42. In Madagascar, the inner skins of leaves are peeled and then stretched out in the tropical sun, which dries and bleaches them.
43. While Henry was swimming at his local pool, the lights suddenly went off.
44. When it was announced that the fancy-dress competition was about to take place, we huddled together to plan our escape.
45–52. Refer to Paper 1 Q11–18 on plurals.
45. **punches** As the word ends in 'ch', 'es' needs to be added.
46. **buses** As the word ends in 's', 'es' needs to be added.
47. **sausages** The letter 's' just needs to be added.
48. **convoys** The letter 's' just needs to be added.
49. **dresses** As the word ends in 'ss', 'es' needs to be added.
50. **waltzes** As the word ends in 'z', 'es' needs to be added.
51. **tariffs** The letter 's' just needs to be added.
52. **thieves** The 'f' needs to be removed and replaced with 'ves'.
53–60. Refer to Paper 2 Q11–17 on nouns.
Daisy, **Daisy**, / Give me your **answer** do, / I'm half crazy / All for the **love** of you; / It won't be a stylish **marriage**, / For I can't afford a **carriage** – / But you'll look sweet / Upon the **seat** / Of a **bicycle** made for two!
61–64. 'What do we do now?' grumbled Jay through gritted teeth. 'They're bound to sabotage our camp.'
'They can't do anything until it gets dark,' consoled Mimi. 'We'll just have to make sure we stay up all through the night.'
65–68. 'I'm frozen,' complained Jay. 'It really is cold and dark,' he sighed. 'Maybe they aren't going to come back tonight.'
Mimi considered Jay's comment. 'But maybe they will!' she replied.

69 glass
70 gladiator
71 gesture
72 globe
73 gold
74 gnat
75 gradient
76 garbage

77–86 Homophones are words that are pronounced the same but have a different meaning or spelling.

77–78 **boy, buoy** The boy untied his boat from the buoy.
79–80 **fare, fair** The fare for a ride at the fair was £3.00.
81–82 **knew, new** Jason knew his new jeans would fit perfectly.
83–84 **sure, shore** 'Are you sure we can see the shore from here?' asked the children.
85–86 **ewe, yew** The ewe died after eating the yew, a very poisonous plant.

87–94 Reported speech tells us about what someone has said and does not use inverted commas. Direct speech tells us the exact words that have been spoken and those words needs to surrounded by inverted commas.

Kate's dad called to her to hurry up.
'Hurry up Kate!' called Dad.
Sarah explained to Pete she was going on holiday soon.
'Pete, I'm going on holiday soon,' explained Sarah.
The Singh family yelled to the passing boat that they needed help.
'Help!' yelled the Singh family to the passing boat.
Mum asked her friend if she thought it might rain today.
'Do you think it might rain today?' Mum asked her friend.

95–100 A diminutive is a word that describes a smaller version of something.

95 piglet
96 booklet
97 duckling
98 hillock
99 owlet
100 statuette

Paper 4 (pages 17–23)

1 **Cedric**
2 **was happy** (lines 10–11)
3 **eyebrows**
4 *When seeing Lord Fauntleroy, Mrs Mellon made reference to his father, 'the Captain', so she must have known him (lines 7–8).*
5 *It was a great day because Lord Fauntleroy was the heir and he had come to live at his estate (lines 18–19).*
6 *He didn't want Lord Fauntleroy to overhear what he said.*
7 *Lord Fauntleroy had been acknowledged by the dog, though not immediately by his grandfather.*
8–9 *The passage talks about many staff like the housekeeper, footman, etc.; reference is made by Mrs Mellon to the nursery upstairs.*
10 *He was delighted/excited about meeting his grandchild and was struck by his confidence, which caught him unawares.*
11 The dogs **race** after the ball.
12 Ben **stirs** the cake mixture.
13 The chick learns to **scratch** the earth.
14 The Head Teacher **sings** loudly and clearly during assembly.
15 The rain **pours** down on the washing hung on the line.
16 Rashid **peels** a banana.
17 The duck **feeds** greedily on the bread.
18–27 A compound word is a word made up of two separate words. For example, *tooth* and *brush* can be put together to form the word *toothbrush*. Here are some possible answers:
18–19 *tablecloth, tabletop*
20–21 *anywhere, anytime*
22–23 *snowball, snowman*
24–25 *handbag, handshake*
26–27 *something, someone*
28–33 An adjective is a word that describes a noun, such as *yellow, large, excited,* or *sweet*. Here are some possible answers:
28 *colourful*
29 *wooden*
30 *strict*
31 *naughty*
32 *new*
33 *noisy*
34 Possible answers include: *piccolo, flute, whistle, kazoo, oboe*
35 **volcano**
36 **umbrella**
37 **shampoo**
38 **confetti**
39 **pizza**

ANSWERS

40–45 Adverbials of time describe when and how long something happens. Examples of adverbials of time are: *last week, soon, since Tuesday.* Adverbials of place (also called preposition phrases) describe where something happens. Examples are: *everywhere, towards the door, away,* etc. Refer to Paper 1 Q25–31 on question marks and exclamation marks.

46–52 Words that have the same spelling patterns will have either a small group of letters the same or a silent letter the same.
46 experience – license
47 thorough – borough
48 performance – balance
49 plumber – numbness
50 entrant – instant
51 present – agent
52 electrician – optician
53 **past** The word 'walked' shows us that the action happened in the past.
54 **future** The words 'am going to' tell us the action will be in the future.
55 **past** The word 'wrote' shows us that the action happened in the past.
56 **present** The words 'am sipping' show us that the action is happening now.
57 **past** The words 'have made' show us that the action happened in the past.
58 **future** The words 'will tidy' show us that the action will be in the future.
59 **present** The words 'am typing' show us that the action is happening now.

60–67 If the root word ends in a consonant followed by a 'y' then the 'y' is changed to 'i' and 'ful' is added. For all other words 'ful' just needs to be added. However, some words are an exception to this rule.
60 **thoughtful** The suffix 'ful' just needs to be added.
61 **awful** The 'e' is removed before the suffix 'ful' is added.
62 **pitiful** The 'y' changes to an 'i' before the suffix 'ful' is added.
63 **deceitful**
64 **shameful**
65 **merciful**
66 **hopeful**
67 **dreadful**

68–75 A conjunction is a word that is used to join a main clause and a subordinate clause together in a sentence. Refer to Paper 3 Q38–44 on clauses and conjunctions.
68 *although* or *even though*
69 *because* or *as*
70 *so*
71 *but*
72 *and*
73 *since*
74 *until*
75 *because* or *as*

76–82 An onomatopoeic word is a word that describes a sound. The sound of the word imitates the sound being described, for example: hiss, sizzle, pop, or bang.
76 lion
77 sheep
78 pig
79 turkey
80 cat
81 hen
82 dog

83–92 Refer to Paper 1 Q47–54 on pronouns.
83–84 **We** must buy **him** a packet as well.
85–87 Where is **mine**? Have **you** got **it**?
88–89 **His** is longer than **yours**.
90 Why are **theirs** the same?
91–92 **I** wonder what **they** are doing.

93–100 When adding 'able' or 'ible' to a word there is no set rule. However, the suffix 'able' is much more common. If the last letter is 'e', this will sometimes need to be removed before the suffix is added.
93 adorable
94 noticeable
95 collapsible
96 accessible
97 desirable
98 reversible
99 sensible
100 movable

Paper 5 (pages 23–28)

1 **water** (line 1)
2 **97%** (line 14)
3 **clear** (line 22)
4 It is described as a recycling process because the same water is changed into something else (water vapour) then back into liquid water again so it is reused.
5 shows an image of something, mirrors
6–7 Acceptable answers could include two of the following points: *Salts are washed off the land. Salt escapes from cracks in the ocean floor. Salts come from undersea volcanoes.*
8–9 **bullet point three** *It fits best here because this section discusses water and its use and effect on living things.*
10 *How important for life is water?*
11–18 A preposition is a word that tells us how one thing relates to another. They are words that tell us the position, direction or time of something.

11	in
12	behind
13	among
14	up
15	through
16	down
17–18	on, up
19	plane
20	hanky
21	head
22	paper
23	champ
24	exam
25–31	When the root word ends in a vowel, then the suffix 'cial' is used. When the root word ends in a consonant, 'tial' is used. The root words have been given below wherever possible.
25	**cial** commercial (The root word is 'commerce'.)
26	**tial** partial (The root word is 'part'.)
27	**tial** confidential (The root word is 'confident'.)
28	**cial** artificial (The root word is 'artifice'.)
29	**tial** initial (There is no root word for 'initial', so this spelling needs to be learned separately.)
30	**cial** special (There is no root word for 'special', so this spelling needs to be learned separately.)
31	**cial** financial (The root word is 'finance'.)
32–38	Refer to Paper 1 Q40–46 on synonyms. Possible answers:
32	*questioned*
33	*noise*
34	*unexciting*
35	*choice*
36	*inspected*
37	*tight*
38	*great*
39–42	'What time does the party start?' Helen called.
43–49	'We must concentrate,' said David. 'If we don't get this work done we'll have to miss our playtime.'
50–55	Refer to Paper 1 Q32–39 on letter strings.
50	height
51	barn
52	stove
53	head
54	glove
55	plead
56–61	A double negative is when two words meaning 'no' are used in a sentence, which makes its meaning confusing or unclear.
56	**Jake hasn't walked a half-marathon.**
57	**There wasn't any milk left by the milkman.**
58	**Cath hasn't a drink for her lunch.** 'Hasn't got a' or 'Has no' could be used in place of 'hasn't a'.
59	**Dad's not ever going there again.** 'Never' could be used in place of 'not ever'.
60	**There aren't any red squirrels here.** 'Are no' can be used in place of 'aren't any'.
61	**I don't have enough money to buy that.**
62–69	Refer to Paper 3 Q77–86 on homophones.
62	**sight** or **cite**
63	**border**
64	**hoarse**
65	**stationery**
66	**flour**
67	**sure**
68	**waive**
69	**Sunday**
70–79	Refer to Paper 2 Q54–59 on powerful verbs.
70–71	*raced, somersaulted*
72–73	*dived, screamed*
74–75	*sprint, yelled*
76–77	*struggled, glimpse*
78–79	*tripped, gasped*
80–86	(1) **Norfolk**, (2) **Northumberland**, (3) **Nottinghamshire**, (4) **Somerset**, (5) **South Glamorgan**, (6) **Strathclyde**, (7) **Suffolk**
87–92	Conjunctions are words that join two main clauses together in a sentence.
87	Ella had to sit down for tea **even though** her favourite programme was on.
88	Daniel needed his boots **but** he couldn't find them.
89	The runner stopped the race **after** he hurt his ankle.
90	Veejay handed in his homework **although** it was past the deadline.
91	The kittens drank their milk and chased the ball **before** settling down for the night.
92	It was time for Jane to go home **though** she wanted to stay longer.
93–100	knowledge, garage, imagine, refugee, generous, dungeon, gigantic, message

Paper 6 (pages 29–34)

1	**November** (line 4)
2	**a horse** (e.g. line 12, 'nickering gently to him')
3	*Albert had not been himself since David, obviously a close friend or relative, had died.*
4	*It was at that moment the end of the war had arrived. It was the eleventh hour of the eleventh month.*
5	*whinnying*
6–7	profound – *deep, intense* jauntily – *cheerfully*
8–9	*Albert had become sad, quiet and unhappy. This is shown when the author says that he no longer smiled or joked and that even when he knew that the war was ending, there was no light in his eyes.*

ANSWERS

10 He knew that his men cared deeply for the horses, as shown in the relationship between Albert and Joey, and he knew this would be bad news for them.

11–18 Refer to Paper 2 Q11–17 on collective nouns.
- 11 **herd**
- 12 **flock** or **herd**
- 13 **litter**
- 14 **colony**
- 15 **school** or **shoal**
- 16 **pride**
- 17 **swarm**
- 18 **flock**

19–24 A relative clause gives you extra information about the noun or verb it relates to. The sentence needs to include the relative pronoun given in each question. Question 24 needs to be a sentence that has had the relative pronoun left out. For example: *This is the present I bought today.*

25–33 Unfortunately, there is no set rule to help with adding the suffixes 'ory', 'ary' or 'ery' to these particular words and these spellings have to be learnt individually.
- 25 **ary** February
- 26 **ary** dictionary
- 27 **ory** history
- 28 **ery** mystery
- 29 **ary** ordinary
- 30 **ary** secretary
- 31 **ery** jewellery
- 32 **ary** necessary
- 33 **ory** memory

34–40 When words have been shortened, apostrophes are added to show where letters have been removed. These are also referred to as contractions.
- 34 **Don't go over there!**
- 35 **We could've gone to the beach.**
- 36 **They'll be home soon.**
- 37–38 **It's time to go to ballet, isn't it?**
- 39 **I shan't eat my tea!**
- 40 **We'll buy some sweets tomorrow.**
- 41 **ghost**
- 42 **rat**
- 43 **head**
- 44 **cart**
- 45 **heart**
- 46 **bush**
- 47 **apple**

48–58 In book titles, the first word and all other words should be capitalised. The only words that are not capitalised are prepositions (of, in, etc) and determiners (a, an, the, etc), Conjunctions such as 'and' are also not capitalised.

48–50 **Classic Children's Stories**
51–54 **The Little Book of Facts**
55–58 **Keeping Ponies Season by Season**
59–65 Refer to the following: Paper 2 Q40–45 on verbs; Paper 1 Q47–54 on pronouns; Paper 2 Q11–17 on nouns; Paper 5 Q11–18 on prepositions; Paper 4 Q28–33 on adjectives; and Paper 3 Q38–44 on conjunctions. An adverb is a word that describes a verb; it describes how something has happened.
- 59 **bounce**
- 60 **they**
- 61 **tree**
- 62 **greedily**
- 63 **under**
- 64 **lank**
- 65 **although**
- 66 **I was going swimming.** 'Was going' can be replaced with 'went'.
- 67 **The thunder was frightening.**
- 68 **The children were going to pick blackberries.** 'Were going to pick' can be replaced with 'picked' or 'went to pick'.
- 69 **My gran was living on her own.** 'Was living' can be replaced with 'lived'.
- 70 **The dog was swimming in the pond.** 'Was swimming' can be replaced with 'swam'.
- 71 **The school orchestra was practising.** 'Was practising' can be replaced with 'practised'.

72–75 **Internet, website, email, DVD**
76–79 Refer to Paper 1 Q40–46 on synonyms.
- 76 **ignore**
- 77 **annoy**
- 78 **reassure**
- 79 **reply**

80–85 Auxiliary verbs are used with a main verb to show which tense the sentence is in. Examples of auxiliary verbs are: am, are, were, will, be, can, etc.
- 80 The horse **was** racing towards the sea.
- 81 The pigs **are** guzzling down their swill.
- 82 The jewels **are** discovered by the thieves.
- 83 James **is** running in the relay race.
- 84 The telephone **was** ringing.
- 85 Fern's class **were/was** going to read to the younger children.

86–92 Words with a soft 'c' sound have the letter 'c' pronounced as an 's'. In most cases the 'c' in the word is followed by the letter 'e', 'i' or 'y'. **innocent, centimetre, electricity, sequence, practice, peace, fancy**

93–100 Refer to Paper 2 Q60–68 on root words.
- 93 **agree**able The suffix 'able' has been added.
- 94 **direct**ion The suffix 'tion' has been added.
- 95 **force**ful The suffix 'ful' has been added.
- 96 **mis**match The prefix 'mis' has been added.

97 **optional** The suffix 'al' has been added.
98 **reloading** The prefix 're' and the suffix 'ing' have been added.
99 **dis**coloured The prefix 'dis' and the suffix 'ed' have been added.
100 **tiresome** The suffix 'some' has been added.

Paper 7 (pages 34–40)

1 **winter** (e.g. 'snow', line 16)
2 **to guide her home with a light** (lines 15–16)
3 **no** (line 32)
4 *It was just past two in the afternoon and he thought the storm wasn't due for many hours* (lines 13, 18, 19).
5–6 Two of: **'She wandered up and down'** (line 30); **'And many a hill did Lucy climb'** (line 31); **'A furlong from their door'** (line 40).
7–8 *They were desperate and upset. This is shown when the poet says that they were 'wretched' and they 'wept'* (lines 33 and 41).
9–10 *the language the poem is written in (using words such as 'oft', 'dwelt' and 'yonder'; the fact Lucy was carrying a lantern rather than a torch*
11–15 'There' tells us where something is; 'their' tells us who something belongs to; 'they're' is a short form of 'they are'.
11 **their** The Jacob family were on their way home.
12–13 **They're, their** They're all very tired after their late night.
14–15 **there, they're** The chocolate biscuits are there but remember they're for everyone!
16–20 'Two' means the number two; 'to' tells us the direction or position of something, or the relationship of one thing to another, or can be part of a verb; 'too' means 'as well' or 'overly'.
16–17 **to, to** Dad had to walk to the station this morning.
18–19 **two, too** Dave has had two days off school and he is not too well again today.
20 **too** Mum is going to buy some dog food but I need to remind her she needs some cat food too.
21–26 A noun phrase is a small group of words that contain one or more adjectives (words that describe a noun).
21 Freda, the **long-haired, cream-coloured** cat, slept soundly.
22 Florence loved her **thick, long, dark** hair.
23 Jim dived through the **sticky, wet** mud, saving the goal.
24 The friends burned while playing in the **blistering, scorching** heat of the sun.
25 The baby-sitter told **exciting, but scary and often terrifying, late night** stories!

26 The **glistening, coloured** vase shimmered in the sunlight.
27 **skin and blister – sister**
28 **apples and pears – stairs**
29 **bread and cheese – knees**
30 **plates of meat – feet**
31 **sugar and honey – money**
32 **frog and toad – road**
33–40 Refer to Paper 1 Q40–46 on synonyms. Here are some possible answers.
33 *amusing, funny*
34 *change, alter*
35 *dull, tedious*
36 *hide, conceal*
37 *sway, stumble*
38 *pull, yank*
39 *strange, unknown*
40 *damage, deface*
41–58 'Listen everyone, I have an announcement to make,' shouted Mr Bridges above the noise. 'I've arranged for us all to camp out at Harlington Hall. We will see for ourselves if it is haunted or not!'
The colour faded from Hannah's face.
59–66 If a word ends in a vowel followed by a 'y' then 's' just needs to be added. If a word ends in a consonant followed by a 'y' then the 'y' is removed and 'ies' is added.
59 **armies** The letter 'y' is removed and replaced with 'i' and 'es' is added.
60 **quantities**
61 **trolleys** The letter 's' just needs to be added.
62 **cowboys**
63 **novelties**
64 **responsibilities**
65 **stairways**
66 **remedies**
67–73 An abbreviation is a word that has been shortened. An acronym is formed from the initial letters of a group of words.
67 **CID**
68 **km**
69 **DIY**
70 **UN**
71 **UFO**
72 **VIP**
73 **e.g.** or **eg**
74–79 A hyphen is needed between a prefix and a root word, such as when the prefix ends in a vowel and the root word begins with a vowel, e.g. co-own needs a hyphen as 'coown' will not make sense. Here are some possible answers: *co-ordinate, re-enter, co-own, cross-country, co-author, co-star, ex-directory.*
80–85 Refer to Paper 3 Q87–94 on indirect speech.

80 Sarah enquired what time we should meet.
81 A hungry boy exclaimed that it must be lunchtime.
82 Tony moaned that he wished he didn't have so much work to do.
83 The park keeper called out that dogs weren't allowed in the park.
84 Mum shouted that I should clear up my room.
85 Jane asked whether I had checked out that website.
86 **soreness** The suffix 'ness' just needs to be added with no change to the root word.
87 **regardless** The suffix 'less' just needs to be added with no change to the root word.
88 **plentiful** The 'y' is replaced with 'i' and the suffix 'ful' is added.
89 **achievement** The suffix 'ment' just needs to be added with no change to the root word.
90 **examination** The 'e' is changed to an 'a' and the suffix 'tion' is added.
91 **shapeless** The suffix 'less' just needs to be added with no change to the root word.
92 **stressful** The suffix 'ful' just needs to be added with no change to the root word.
93 **tiresome** The suffix 'some' just needs to be added with no change to the root word.
94–100 Refer to Paper 5 Q87–92 on conjunctions. Possible answers:
94 *although, until*
95 *where*
96 *because, as*
97 *but*
98 *as, because*
99 *when*
100 *after*

Paper 8 (pages 41–45)

1 **600 million** (line 5)
2 **money each month to support their work** (line 2)
3–4 *It helps the sponsors give the children and their families things they need such as clean water. Providing a school for boys and girls, a medical centre or an income generating scheme are also acceptable answers (lines 20–21).*
5 **community leaders, parents and the children themselves** (lines 18–19)
6 *An 'income-generating scheme' is one which provides skills and supplies to enable families to support themselves.*
7 *polluted/unclean*
8 *It means that each child is capable of leading a rich and successful life.*
9–10 Acceptable answers could include: *by giving examples of the problems; by naming some children who need help; by explaining how people can help.*
11–18 If the root word ends in 'ce', remove the 'e' and add 'ious' (for example, 'space' becomes 'spacious'). If the root word ends in 'city', remove the 'ty' and add 'ous' (for example, 'ferocity' becomes 'ferocious'). If the root word ends in 'tion', remove 'ion' and add 'ious' (for example, 'nutrition' becomes 'nutritious'). However, there are exceptions to these rules: in this case words like suspicious, bumptious and scrumptious.
11 **tious** ambitious (The root word is 'ambition', so 'ion' is replaced with 'ious'.)
12 **cious** delicious (There is no root word for 'delicious' so this spelling needs to be learned separately.)
13 **tious** bumptious (This is an exception to the rule as 't' needs to be added, followed by 'ious'.)
14 **tious** scrumptious
15 **cious** tenacious (The root word is 'tenacity', so 'ty' is removed and 'ous' is added.)
16 **cious** suspicious
17 **tious** infectious (The root word is 'infect', so 'ion' is removed and 'ious' is added.)
18 **cious** ferocious (The root word is 'ferocity', so 'ty' is removed and 'ous' is added.)
19–26 Refer to Paper 3 Q38–44 on commas.
19–20 The coat lining felt odd, sort of lumpy, and I thought I could hear a faint squeak coming from inside it.
21 As it came nearer, it slowly took on the form of a boat.
22 A dreaded monster lived in the castle nearby, watching over the townsfolk's every move.
23 Rick and James began to argue, each blaming the other for the broken window.
24 You know what it is like, you try to work but you find yourself staring out the window.
25–26 Sam, who was hungry after playing football, was glad to see his mum making sandwiches.
27 **billy-goat**
28 **hero**
29 **count**
30 **gander**
31 **stag or buck**
32 **nephew**
33–39 Refer to Paper 6 Q59–65 on adverbs. **quickly, impatiently, hurriedly, excitedly, diligently, undeniably, constantly, soon, always**
40–49 Refer to Paper 2 Q18–25 on antonyms.
40–41 *love, desire*
42–43 *run, sprint*
44–45 *small, tiny*

46–47 *calm, still*
48–49 *dark, dim or heavy, weighty*
  50 **confetti**
  51 **volcano**
  52 **spaghetti**
  53 **shampoo**
  54 **umbrella**
  55 **cello**
56–64

	er	est	ish
large	larger	largest	largish
sweet	sweeter	sweetest	sweetish
cold	colder	coldest	coldish

65–71 Refer to Paper 5 Q11–18 on prepositions.
  65 *under*
  66 *onto*
  67 *over*
68–69 *through, along*
  70 *around*
  71 *in*
72–75 'It's time we set off on holiday,' called Mum.
76–82 'Where is my coat?' shouted Danny. 'It is too cold to go outside without it.'
  83 **ballet – France**
  84 **karate – Japan**
  85 **dachshund – Germany**
  86 **bravo – Italy**
  87 He/she/(person's name)/they fainted with the pain.
  88 He/she/(person's name)/they eats quickly.
  89 He/she/(person's name)/they fell down the stairs.
  90 They/(people's names)/they love playing computer games.
  91 He's/she's/(person's name)'s/they're walking the dog.
  92 They're/(people's names)'re going to see a film.
93–94 It **was** time to go to bed but they **were** not tired.
  95 What **is** Dad going to do about the broken door?
  96 When **are** the spring bulbs going to appear?
  97 The phone rang when we **were** outside.
98–99 The volcano **is** erupting as the villagers **are** sleeping.
 100 When **are** we going swimming?

Paper 9 (pages 46–51)

  1 **a hillside of loose stones** (line 1)
  2 **no** (lines 8–9)
  3 **loose stones** (lines 25–26)
  4 *He had two helpings of goat.*
  5 *vast, huge, extensive*
  6 *It suggests Edmund doesn't have much time for Eustace and is irritated by him.*
  7 *because on closer inspection he realised how treacherous the path was* (lines 13–17)
  8 *because he hadn't read stories with dragons in or previously been told about them like most children* (lines 28–29)
9–10 Child's answer describing their interpretation of how Eustace felt, e.g. scared, terrified, cautious but relieved he hadn't yet been noticed. Eustace felt frightened before he saw the dragon. This is shown in the line 'It froze him dead still where he stood for a second' (line 21). (This line occurs when he *hears* the dragon, *before* he has seen it.)
11–18 Refer to Paper 1 questions 11–18 and Paper 7 questions 59–66.
  11 **scarves** The 'f' is replaced with 'v' and 'es' is added.
  12 **wolves**
  13 **beliefs** Unlike other words that end in 'f', 'belief' is an exception to the rule and 's' just needs to be added.
  14 **handcuffs** The letter 's' just needs to be added.
  15 **wives** 'fe' is removed and 'ves' is added.
  16 **penknives**
  17 **remedies** The 'y' is replaced with 'i' and 'es' is added.
  18 **motifs**
  19 Brian couldn't find **anything** to watch on TV.
  20 'There is **nothing** to eat,' moaned Tracey.
  21 The bag had **nothing** in it.
22–23 The twins called, 'There is **nothing** to do. We can't find **anything** to play with.'
  24 Orin said the mess was **nothing** to do with him.
  25 'I'll read **anything** to fill the time,' said Kate.
  26 *a bad dream*
  27 *a piece of anything left over*
  28 *to move slowly*
  29 *a short rush of strong wind*
  30 *brave*
  31 *a carefully thought-out idea that is not yet proven*
  32 *horrible, very unpleasant*
  33 The Gallop family **were** having a day out.
  34 Nasar **will** pack his bag.
  35 Hannah and David **were** planning to have a sleepover.
  36 Ben left in a hurry but **was** there just in time.
  37 We **shall** climb the apple tree when we get home.
  38 They **were** going on holiday.
  39 The girls **are** leaning against the shop window.
  40 After the water fight, Hugh **was** soaking.

ANSWERS

41–45 Refer to Paper 6 Q59–65 on adverbs. Each of the listed adverbs used correctly in different sentences. For example, *The team waited anxiously as the ball flew towards the goal.*

46–56 Refer to Paper 3 Q38–44 on commas.

46–48 On a bright, warm day, we like to go to the park.

49–52 When I play with Jack, my pet dog, I usually get tired before he does.

53–56 Nina bought some pens, pencils, rubbers and a ruler before the first day of school.

57–63 Refer to Paper 2 Q18–25 on antonyms.
- 57 downs
- 58 thick
- 59 black
- 60 going
- 61 rough
- 62 less
- 63 near
- 64 excellent
- 65 separate
- 66 marvellous
- 67 bruise
- 68 category
- 69 individual
- 70 twelfth
- 71 restaurant

72–77 Refer to Paper 2 Q40–45 on clauses.

72–73 <u>I ran quickly up the street</u> as Aunty Sam had arrived.

74–75 <u>Helga put on her boots</u> because she loved to splash in puddles.

76–77 <u>Guy walked off in the opposite direction</u> after he lost his tennis match to Hussan.

78–85 Refer to Paper 4 Q46–52 on spelling patterns.
- 78 *drain*
- 79 *tough*
- 80 *blouse*
- 81 *rumble*
- 82 *relate, ultimatum*
- 83 *funnel*
- 84 *lord, chorus*
- 85 *universe, diverge*

86–92 Refer to the following: Paper 1 Q63–70 on nouns; Paper 4 Q28–33 on adjectives; Paper 2 Q40–45 on verbs; and Paper 1 Q71–77 on suffixes. To change nouns into adjectives, the following suffixes have been used: 'ise', 'ify' and 'ate'.

- 86 **dramatise** As the last letter in 'drama' is 'a', 't' is added, followed by 'ise'.
- 87 **magnetise** or **magnify** To form the word 'magnetise', the suffix 'ise' just needs to be added. To form the word 'magnify', remove 'et' and add the suffix 'ify'.
- 88 **specialise** The suffix 'ise' just needs to be added as the word ends in a consonant.
- 89 **economise** The 'y' is removed and the suffix 'ise' is added.
- 90 **terrorise**
- 91 **verbalise**
- 92 **alienate** The suffix 'ate' just needs to be added.

93–94 Refer to Paper 4 Q28–33 on adjectives.
- **93–94** slower, slowest
- **95–96** less, least
- **97–98** farther/further, farthest/furthest
- **99–100** larger, largest

Paper 10 (pages 52–57)

1 **Helios** The introductory text tells us that Helios is the 'Greek sun god'.
2 **let the horses guide him** (line 1)
3 **was hit by a thunderbolt** (line 35)
4 *Phaeton was keen to show those on Earth that he was the son of a god; to impress his friends.*
5–6 *He thinks about himself but not others. This is shown when he ignores his father's warning and steers the chariot towards Earth just because he wants everyone to see him.*
7 A metaphor is a phrase that is used to give a more detailed description. It is used to compare an object or person to something with similar characteristics. Whereas in a simile the words 'like' or 'as' are used, in a metaphor the words 'is', 'was', 'are', 'am', etc are used. For example, 'the sun is a golden coin'. Acceptable answers could include any of the following:
'Light began to climb into the dark sky and the restless horses leaped into the waiting blackness'; 'the wheels and the hooves made splinters of light which surrounded the chariot like a ball of fire'; 'He looked over the side and thought of the people woken by rays from the sun chariot'; the various lines in which the horses send fire to Earth.
8 *unproductive, with few plants or animals*
9 *burnt*
10 *It is always worth listening to, and being prepared to heed, the advice of those who are more experienced than oneself.*

11–18 Refer to Paper 2 Q18–25 on prefixes.
- 11 **overact** or **react**
- 12 **miscount** or **recount**
- 13 **discharge, recharge** or **overcharge**
- 14 **overbalance**
- 15 **misbehave**

16 **retouch**
17 **retrace**
18 **disbelieve**
19–25 Apostrophes are used to show who or what something belongs to. When it belongs to one person or thing, the word ends in an apostrophe followed by an 's' ('s). When it belongs to more than one, then 's' is added followed by an apostrophe (s').
19 Ben's football had a puncture.
20 They were thirsty, but the cows' water trough was empty.
21 It suddenly rained and the three girls' coats were soaked.
22 Mark's finger hurt after he shut it in a car door!
23 Aunty Sue's family waved as they turned the corner.
24 Dan lost his ticket for football's greatest match, the Cup Final.
25 Five groups' designs were displayed in the school hall.
26–31 Refer to Paper 2 Q18–25 on antonyms.
wall, London, yellow, diamond, month, egg
32–36 Refer to Paper 3 Q87–94 on indirect speech.
32 The teacher called out that we should not forget that we had homework tonight. ('They' can also be used instead of 'we'. 'should could be 'must' and 'had' could be 'have'.)
33 The tourist asked where the nearest toilet was.
34 The boy screamed that he was caught in the barbed wire.
35 Greg shouted to stop the ball as it was heading for the goal.
36 Seeta mumbled to her best friend that she really didn't like Mondays.
37–48 Refer to the following: Paper 2 Q11–17 on nouns; Paper 1 Q47–54 on pronouns; and Paper 5 Q11–18 on prepositions.

noun	pronoun	preposition
chickens	it	for
night	they	to
pen	he	from
Jordan	them	with
potato		into
meal		
home		

49 ✗
50 ✓
51 ✓
52 ✗
53 ✗
54 ✓
55 ✗
56 ✓
57–71 Sasha's eyes stared in disbelief. Standing quietly in a stable was her very own pony. 'I don't believe he's mine,' she whispered. Her mother smiled because she knew Sasha deserved him.
72–77 Refer to Paper 7 Q67–73 on abbreviations and acronyms.
72 **OAP**
73 **cm**
74 **GB**
75 **HQ**
76 **PM**
77 **PC**
78–83 Child's own phrases added to the gaps in the sentences, e.g. *Tom washed his hands in the <u>warm and soapy</u> water.* Refer to Paper 7 Q21–26 on noun phrases.
84–86 *crash, clap, bang*
87–89 *clickety-clack, whoosh, chug-chug*
90–92 *splash, scream, gasp*
93–100 If a word has a 'short' vowel sound (as in t<u>a</u>p and h<u>u</u>g), the last letter is doubled before the suffix is added. For example, 'tap' becomes 'tapping'. If it is a 'long' vowel sound (as in f<u>a</u>de and s<u>ea</u>t), the 'silent e' at the end of the word is removed and the suffix is added. For example, 'fade' becomes 'fading'. If there is no 'silent e' and the word has a long vowel sound, the suffix just needs to be added. If a word has a 'short' vowel sound (as in jump, stamp) but ends in two consonants, the suffix just needs to be added. However, there are exceptions to this rule and those words need to be learned separately.
93 **hiding** The 'e' is removed before 'ing' is added.
94 **equipping** The 'p' is doubled before 'ing is added.
95 **picnicking** As the word ends in 'c', 'k' is added followed by 'ing'.
96 **amusing** The 'e' is removed before 'ing' is added.
97 **testing** When a verb ends in two (or more) consonants, you just add 'ing'
98 **enrolling** This is an exception to the rule: the 'l' is doubled and 'ing' is added.
99 **thieving** As the word ends in 'f', this is removed and replaced with 'v', then 'ing' is added.
100 **separating** The 'e' is removed before 'ing' is added.

Paper 11 (pages 58–63)

1. **American** (line 2)
2. **1968** (line 16)
3. **15 months after he set out**
4. *The achievement of making it to the North Pole first.*
5. **'on top of the Earth'** (line 6)
6. *Only fellow explorers are really aware of who he is and what he has achieved.*

7–10. *He is described as the 'explorers' explorer' (lines 13–14); the journey to the North Pole was just one expedition he led (line 22); he mapped about 45,000 square miles of the pole and personally drew maps which explorers still use today (lines 22–24); being called Sir Wally tells us he was knighted (lines 11 and 22).*

11–18. Refer to Paper 4 Q18–27 on compound words. Here are some possible answers.

11–12. *meantime, meanwhile*
13–14. *overdone, overtake, overboard, overnight, overhead, overgrown*
15–16. *weekend, weekday*
17–18. *firewood, fireguard, fireman, firework, fireplace*

19–21. Three sentences each including the listed preposition, e.g. *The cat sat **under** the tree and watched the bird; I placed the mug **in** the cupboard when it was dry; We walked **along** the shore and listened to the sea.*

22–24. Refer to Paper 5 Q11–18 on prepositions. Three of the child's chosen prepositions, such as: *behind, near, up, through, over, before, on, below*

25–34. Capital letters are needed at the beginning of sentences and when writing the name of a person, place or thing (a proper noun) and the personal pronoun I.
Having emptied the larder, Uncle Franklin returned to the rocking chair. He belched loudly, then grinned, trying to make a joke out of it.
Mum walked in, in time to hear the burp.
'Please Frank, don't do that!' she exclaimed.
'Isn't it time you were heading home?'
'I've missed the train,' he explained, 'thought I'd stay longer.'

35–42. Refer to Paper 1 Q40–46 on synonyms. Possible answers.

35. *language, terms*
36. *period, time*
37. *convince*
38. *disruption, disturbance*
39. *dived, jumped*
40. *took*
41. *pushed*
42. *programme, show*

43–48. Refer to Paper 3 Q38–44 on clauses and conjunctions.

43. *as, because, for*
44. *although, but, however*
45. *until*
46. *although, but, however*
47. *so, therefore*
48. *and, so, therefore, while*

49–53. Refer to Paper 5 Q56–61 on double negatives.

49. **There were no parking spaces.** 'Weren't any' can be used in place of 'were no'.
50. **I wasn't going to the park.** 'Was not' can be used instead of 'wasn't'.
51. **We have no money for the fair rides.** 'Haven't any' can be used instead of 'have no'.
52. **There is no chance we'll make it for the start of the match.** 'Isn't a' or 'isn't any' can be used instead of 'is no'.
53. **Jim hasn't bought a new coat.** 'Has not' can be used instead of 'hasn't'.

54–61. To change the word from the plural to the singular, usually the 's' or 'es' is just removed. However, if the word ends in 'ves', then the 'v' is changed to 'f' and 'es' is removed; if the word ends in 'ies', then 'i' is changed to 'y' and 'es' is removed.

54. **safe** The 's' just needs to be removed.
55. **scarf** The 'v' is replaced with 'f' and 'es' is removed.
56. **deer** The plural and singular form are the same.
57. **hero** 'es' just needs to be removed.
58. **sheep**
59. **crocus** 'es' just needs to be removed.
60. **berry** The 'i' needs to be replaced with 'y' and 'es' is removed.
61. **shelf**

62–63. We **were** waiting for Tony who **was** not ready.
64–65. I **was** asked to play the lead role in the play and Sean **was** chosen to play my brother.
66–67. They **were** worried about the match with Forest School as last year they **were** at the top of the league.
68–69. As you **were** late for the film at the cinema I assume it **was** impossible to get tickets?

70–77. Refer to Paper 1 Q71–77 on suffixes. If the root word ends in a vowel followed by 'y', then the suffix just needs to be added. If the root word ends in a consonant followed by 'y', then the 'y' is changed to 'i' and the suffix is added. The same applies if the root word ends with a silent 'e'.

70. **tastier** As the root word 'taste' ends in a silent 'e', the 'e' is replaced with 'i' and 'er' is added.
71. **playful** As the root word 'play' ends in a vowel followed by 'y', the suffix 'ful' just needs to be added.

Rewrite these sentences in the **past tense**.

66 I'm going swimming.

_____

67 The thunder is frightening.

_____

68 The children are going to pick blackberries.

_____

69 My gran is living on her own.

_____

70 The dog is swimming in the pond.

_____

71 The school orchestra are practising.

_____

Underline the four words or terms that have entered our language in the last fifty years.

72–75 Internet   website   automobile   television   email   electricity   telephone   DVD

Underline one word in each group which is not a **synonym** for the rest.

76 respond	acknowledge	ignore	answer	reply
77 charm	cheer	amuse	annoy	delight
78 reassure	worry	agonise	upset	unsettle
79 ask	investigate	quiz	examine	reply

Finish each sentence by adding a helper **verb** to match the **tense** in bold.

80 The horse _____ racing towards the sea.   **past**

81 The pigs _____ guzzling down their swill.   **present**

82 The jewels _____ discovered by the thieves.   **present**

83 James _____ running in the relay race.   **present**

84 The telephone _____ ringing.   **past**

85 Fern's class _____ going to read to the younger children.   **past**

Circle the words which have a soft 'c'.

86–92 innocent centimetre collapse electricity catch sequence
clueless ache practice synchronise fantastic peace
condense fancy alcove

Underline the **root word** of each of these words.

93 agreeable 94 direction 95 forceful
96 mismatch 97 optional 98 reloading
99 discoloured 100 tiresome

Now go to the Progress Chart to record your score! Total 100

Paper 7

Lucy Gray; or, Solitude

Oft I had heard of Lucy Gray:
And, when I crossed the wild,
I chanced to see at break of day
The solitary child.

No mate, no comrade Lucy knew;
She dwelt on a wide moor,
– The sweetest thing that ever grew
Beside a human door!

You yet may spy the fawn at play,
The hare upon the green;
But the sweet face of Lucy Gray
Will never more be seen.

'To-night will be a stormy night –
You to the town must go;
And take a lantern, Child, to light
Your mother through the snow.'

'That, Father! will I gladly do:
'Tis scarcely afternoon –
The minster-clock has just struck two,
And yonder is the moon!'

At this the Father raised his hook,
And snapped a faggot-band;
He plied his work; – and Lucy took
The lantern in her hand.

Not blither is the mountain roe:
With many a wanton stroke
Her feet disperse the powdery snow,
That rises up like smoke.

The storm came on before its time:
She wandered up and down;
And many a hill did Lucy climb:
But never reached the town.

The wretched parents all that night
Went shouting far and wide;
But there was neither sound nor sight
To serve them for a guide.

At day-break on a hill they stood
They overlooked the moor;
And thence they saw the bridge of wood,
A furlong from their door.

They wept – and, turning homeward, cried,
'In heaven we all shall meet;'
– When in the snow the mother spied
The print of Lucy's feet.

Then downwards from the steep hill's edge   45
They tracked the footmarks small;
And through the broken hawthorn hedge,
And by the long-stone wall;

And then an open field they crossed:
The marks were still the same;   50
They tracked them on, nor ever lost;
And to the bridge they came.

They followed from the snowy bank
Those footmarks, one by one,
Into the middle of the plank;   55
And further there were none!

– Yet some maintain that to this day
She is a living child;
That you may see sweet Lucy Gray
Upon the lonesome wild.   60

O'er rough and smooth she trips along,
And never looks behind;
And sings a solitary song
That whistles in the wind.

William Wordsworth

Underline the correct answers.

1 In which season was this poem set?

(summer, autumn, winter)

2 Why was Lucy sent to meet her mother?

(to guide her home with a light, to keep her company on her walk home, to ask her to buy a light before the storm)

3 Did Lucy make it to town before the storm?

(yes, no)

Answer these questions.

4 Why did Lucy's father feel it was safe to send her to town?

_____

_____

5–6 Find two lines in the poem that show Lucy had walked a long way.

_____

_____

_____

7–8 How do you think Lucy's parents felt once they discovered she was missing? Use evidence from the poem to support your answer.

_____

_____

_____

_____

9–10 What evidence is there that this poem was written a long time ago?

_____

_____

_____

Write *there*, *their* or *they're* in each of the gaps.

    11 The Jacob family were on _____ way home.

12–13 _____ all very tired after _____ late night.

14–15 The chocolate biscuits are _____ but remember _____ for everyone!

Write *to*, *too* or *two* in each of the gaps.

16–17 Dad had _____ walk _____ the station this morning.

18–19 Dave has had _____ days off school and he is not _____ well again today.

    20 Mum is going to buy some dog food but I need to remind her she needs some cat food _____.

Underline the **noun phrase** in each sentence.

    21 Freda, the long-haired, cream-coloured cat, slept soundly.

    22 Florence loved her thick, long, dark hair.

    23 Jim dived through the sticky, wet mud, saving the goal.

24 The friends burned while playing in the blistering, scorching heat of the sun.

25 The baby-sitter told exciting, but scary and often terrifying, late night stories!

26 The glistening, coloured vase shimmered in the sunlight.

With a line, match the rhyming slang phrases with their meaning.

27	skin and blister	feet
28	apples and pears	knees
29	bread and cheese	sister
30	plates of meat	road
31	sugar and honey	stairs
32	frog and toad	money

Write a **synonym** for each of these words.

33 humorous _____   34 modify _____

35 monotonous _____   36 camouflage _____

37 stagger _____   38 wrench _____

39 unfamiliar _____   40 vandalise _____

Copy the passage, adding the missing capital letters and punctuation.

41–58 listen everyone I have an announcement to make shouted mr bridges above the noise

ive arranged for us all to camp out at harlington hall we will see for ourselves if it is haunted or not

the colour faded from Hannahs face

Write each of these words in its **plural form**.

59 army _____   60 quantity _____

61 trolley _____   62 cowboy _____

63 novelty _____   64 responsibility _____

65 stairway _____   66 remedy _____

Write the **abbreviations** or **acronyms** of these words.

67 Criminal Investigation Department _____

68 kilometres _____

69 do it yourself _____

70 United Nations _____

71 unidentified flying object _____

72 very important person _____

73 for example _____

74–79 Write six prefixed words that use a hyphen, for example co-operate.

_____   _____

_____   _____

_____   _____

Rewrite these sentences as **indirect speech**.

80 Sarah enquired, 'What time shall we meet?'

_____

81 'It must be lunchtime!' exclaimed a hungry boy.

_____

82 'I wish I didn't have so much work to do,' Tony moaned.

_____

83 The park keeper called out, 'Dogs aren't allowed in this park!'

_____

84 'Clear up your room!' shouted Mum.

_____

85 Jane asked, 'Have you checked out this website?'

_____

Add the **suffix** to each of these words. Don't forget spelling changes.

86 sore + ness = _____

87 regard + less = _____

88 plenty + ful = _____

89 achieve + ment = _____

90 examine + tion = _____

91 shape + less = _____

92 stress + ful = _____

93 tire + some = _____

In each gap, add a different **conjunction**.

94 The soldiers continued to fight _____ they were exhausted.

95 The children finally arrived at the campsite _____ they could set up their tents.

96 George telephoned his Grandad _____ he'd heard he wasn't well.

97 Wang Ling wanted to go out to play _____ she had to finish her story first.

98 Mark was pleased it was football practice _____ it was his favourite sport.

99 Class 6 were cooking _____ they heard the fire alarm.

100 Gaby lost her trainers after she had PE.

Now go to the Progress Chart to record your score! Total ◯ 100

Paper 8

Thinking of sponsoring a child?

Read how for just a small monthly amount you can help bring health and opportunities to children in poor communities.

Every child has potential

There are 600 million children who live on less than 70p a day – that's ten times the UK population.

In Africa, Latin America and large areas of Asia, acute poverty is depriving children of good health. Many children are suffering from avoidable infections or diseases spread through contaminated water.

Trung wants to read An education would be the best start Trung could have in life. But the nearest school is 20 miles away.

Mamadou's family needs seeds Mamadou and his family have a field that could provide food for them but they need seeds, plus advice to help them work their land more effectively.

Amina needs clean water Amina's village only has access to dirty water, so many children's lives are threatened by waterborne illnesses such as dysentery and diarrhoea.

As a sponsor, you can help more children realise that potential

When we begin working with a community, the first thing we do is talk to community leaders, parents and the children themselves to find out what they need most.

It could be access to clean water, a school for both boys and girls, a medical centre or an income-generating scheme so that families can earn a living.

Children represent the future and we believe sponsorship is the best way to help communities. It is children like Trung, Mamadou and Amina who will be able to pass on their knowledge and skills to the next generation.

Taken from a Plan leaflet on sponsoring a child

Underline the correct answers.

1 How many children live on less than 70p a day?

   (1 million, 10 million, 600 million)

2 What is this leaflet asking for?

   (teachers to help educate children, people to talk with village leaders, money each month to support their work)

Answer these questions.

3–4 How does the money provided by the sponsors help the children who need it? Give one example.

_____

_____

_____

5 Who do the charity workers talk to when they first identify a community that needs help?

_____

_____

6 What is meant by 'an income-generating scheme' (line 21)?

_____

_____

7 What is the meaning of the word 'contaminated' on line 9?

_____

8 What is meant by the heading 'Every child has potential' (line 4)?

_____

_____

9–10 Describe two ways the information presented in the leaflet is used to encourage people to become sponsors.

_____

_____

_____

_____

Add *cious* or *tious* to complete each of these words.

11 ambi _____
12 deli _____
13 bump _____
14 scrump _____
15 tena _____
16 suspi _____
17 infec _____
18 fero _____

Add the missing commas to these sentences.

19–20 The coat lining felt odd sort of lumpy and I thought I could hear a faint squeak coming from inside it.

21 As it came nearer it slowly took on the form of a boat.

22 A dreaded monster lived in the castle nearby watching over the townsfolk's every move.

23 Rick and James began to argue each blaming the other for the broken window.

24 You know what it is like you try to work but you find yourself staring out the window.

25–26 Sam who was hungry after playing football was glad to see his mum making sandwiches.

Write the masculine form of each of these words.

27 nanny-goat _____
28 heroine _____
29 countess _____
30 goose _____
31 doe _____
32 niece _____

Underline the **adverbs** in the following passage.

33–39 Henry rushed quickly home after finishing school. He waited impatiently as his mum hurriedly finished her phone conversation.
'Mum, Mum, I've been chosen to narrate the school play,' he said excitedly. 'Mrs Smith says I must work diligently at learning the lines so they can start rehearsals as soon as possible.'
'Well done! I always knew you'd get a part in the play but narrator is undeniably a hard role. You'll have to read through the lines constantly so you know them inside out,' said Mum.

Write two **antonyms** for each word.

40–41 hate _____ _____

42–43 walk _____ _____

44–45 huge _____ _____

46–47 windy _____ _____

48–49 light _____ _____

Add the missing vowels to each of these words.

50 c__nf__tt__ 51 v__lc__n__ 52 sp__gh__tt__

53 sh__mp__ __ 54 umbr__ll__ 55 c__ll__

Complete the table below.

56–64

	er	est	ish
large			
sweet			
cold			

Write a different **preposition** in each gap.

65 Leo hid _____ his bedding.

66 Poppy climbed _____ the hay bales.

67 The sheepdog jumped _____ the gate.

68–69 The train went _____ the tunnel then _____ the sea wall.

70 The teacher walked _____ the playground.

71 Dev snuggled _____ his duvet to keep warm.

Rewrite these sentences and add the missing punctuation.

72–75 It's time we set off on holiday called Mum

_____

76–82 Where is my coat shouted Danny It is too cold to go outside without it

_____

_____

With a line, match the word to the country from where you think it is borrowed.

83 ballet		Germany
84 karate		France
85 dachshund		Japan
86 bravo		Italy

Rewrite each sentence in the third person.

87 I fainted with the pain. _____

88 I eat quickly. _____

89 I fell down the stairs. _____

90 We love playing computer games.

_____

91 I'm walking the dog. _____

92 We're going to see a film.

_____

Underline the correct word in brackets.

93–94 It (was, were) time to go to bed but they (was, were) not tired.

95 What (is, are) Dad going to do about the broken door?

96 When (is, are) the spring bulbs going to appear?

97 The phone rang when we (was, were) outside.

98–99 The volcano (is, are) erupting as the villagers (is, are) sleeping.

100 When (is, are) we going swimming?

Now go to the Progress Chart to record your score!   Total   100

Paper 9

'At last!' said Eustace as he came slithering down a slide of loose stones (*scree*, they call it) and found himself on the level. 'And now, where are those trees? There *is* something dark ahead. Why, I do believe the fog is clearing.'

It was. The light increased every moment and made him blink. The fog lifted. He was utterly in an unknown valley and the sea was nowhere in sight.

At that very moment the others were washing their hands and faces in the river and generally getting ready for dinner and a rest. The work had gone well so far and it was a merry meal. Only after the second helping of goat did Edmund say, 'Where's that blighter Eustace?'

Meanwhile Eustace stared round the unknown valley. It was so narrow and deep, and the precipices which surrounded it so sheer, that it was like a huge pit or trench.

Eustace realised of course that in the fog he had come down the wrong side of the ridge, so he turned at once to see about getting back. But as soon as he had looked he shuddered. Apparently he had by amazing luck found the only possible way down – a long green spit of land, horribly steep and narrow, with precipices on either side. There was no other possible way of getting back. But could he do it, now that he saw what it was really like? His head swam at the very thought of it. He turned round again, thinking that at any rate he'd better have a good drink from the pool first. But as soon as he had turned and before he had taken a step forward into the valley he heard a noise behind him. It was only a small noise but it sounded loud in that immense silence. It froze him dead still where he stood for a second. Then he slewed round his head and looked.

At the bottom of the cliff a little on his left hand was a low, dark hole – the entrance to a cave perhaps. And out of this two thin wisps of smoke were coming. And the loose stones just beneath the dark hollow were moving (that was the noise he had heard) just as if something were crawling in the dark behind them.

Something *was* crawling. Worse still, something was coming out. Edmund or Lucy or you would have recognised it at once, but Eustace had read none of the right books. The thing that came out of the cave was something he had never even imagined – a long lead-coloured snout, dull red eyes, no feathers or fur, a long lithe body that trailed on the ground, legs whose elbows went up higher than its back like a spider's, cruel claws, bat's wings that made a rasping noise on the stones, yards of tail. And the two lines of smoke were coming from its two nostrils. He never said the word *Dragon* to himself. Nor would it have made things any better if he had. But perhaps if he had known something about dragons he would have been a little surprised at this dragon's behaviour. It did not sit up and clap its wings, nor did it shoot out a stream of flame from its mouth. The smoke from its nostrils was like the smoke of a fire that will not last much longer. Nor did it seem to have noticed Eustace.

From *The Chronicles of Narnia: Voyage of the Dawn Treader* by C S Lewis

Underline the correct answers.

1. What is 'scree'?
   (a hillside of loose stones, a level area, another word for 'fog')
2. Was Eustace missed by the group immediately?
   (yes, no)
3. What was the noise Eustace had heard?
   (a fire crackling, his beating heart, loose stones)

Answer these questions.

4. How do we know that Edmund was hungry?

_____

_____

5. What is the meaning of the word 'immense' on line 21?

_____

6. What does the line 'Where's that blighter Eustace?' (lines 8–9) suggest Edmund's relationship with Eustace is like?

_____

_____

7. Why did Eustace hesitate about returning back up the ridge?

_____

_____

8. Why did Eustace not recognise the strange 'thing' as a dragon?

_____

_____

9–10. Describe in your own words how Eustace felt on seeing the dragon and why. Use evidence from the passage to support your answer.

_____

_____

_____

_____

Write each of these words in their **plural** form.

11 scarf _____   12 wolf _____

13 belief _____   14 handcuff _____

15 wife _____   16 penknife _____

17 remedy _____   18 motif _____

Add *anything* or *nothing* to each of these sentences.

19 Brian couldn't find _____ to watch on TV.

20 'There is _____ to eat,' moaned Tracey.

21 The bag had _____ in it.

22–23 The twins called, 'There is _____ to do. We can't find _____ to play with.'

24 Orin said the mess was _____ to do with him.

25 'I'll read _____ to fill the time,' said Kate.

Write a **definition** for each of these words.

26 nightmare _____

27 remnant _____

28 dawdle _____

29 gust _____

30 valiant _____

31 theory _____

32 ghastly _____

Underline the correct word in brackets.

33 The Gallop family (was, were) having a day out.
34 Nasar (have, will) pack his bag.
35 Hannah and David (will, were) planning to have a sleepover.
36 Ben left in a hurry but (was, were) there just in time.
37 We (have, shall) climb the apple tree when we get home.
38 They (will, were) going on holiday.
39 The girls (are, was) leaning against the shop window.
40 After the water fight, Hugh (was, were) soaking.

Write each of these **adverbs** in a sentence.

41 anxiously

_____

42 fully

_____

43 soon

_____

44 wearily

_____

45 somewhere

_____

Copy these sentences and add the missing punctuation and capital letters.

46–48 on a bright warm day we like to go to the park

_____

_____

49–52 when I play with Jack my pet dog I usually get tired before he does

_____

_____

_____

53–56 nina bought some pens pencils rubbers and a ruler before the first day of school

_____

_____

Complete each expression with an **antonym**.

57 ups and _____

58 through _____ and thin

59 _____ and white

60 coming and _____

61 take the _____ with the smooth

62 more or _____

63 _____ and far

Spell each of these words correctly.

64 exselent   _____   65 seperate   _____

66 marvelous   _____   67 briuse   _____

68 categry   _____   69 indivdual   _____

70 twelth   _____   71 resturant   _____

Underline the two **clauses** in each sentence.

72–73 I ran quickly up the street as Aunty Sam had arrived.

74–75 Helga put on her boots because she loved to splash in puddles.

76–77 Guy walked off in the opposite direction after he lost his tennis match to Hussan.

Next to each word write another word with the same spelling pattern.

78 strain   _____   79 rough   _____

80 rouse   _____   81 stumble   _____

82 ultimate   _____   83 tunnel   _____

84 chord   _____   85 diverse   _____

Change each of these **nouns** or **adjectives** into a **verb** by adding a **suffix**.

86 drama _____

87 magnet _____

88 special _____

89 economy _____

90 terror _____

91 verbal _____

92 alien _____

Complete the following **adjectives** of comparison.

Example: quiet   quieter   quietest

93–94 slow _____ _____

95–96 little _____ _____

97–98 far _____ _____

99–100 large _____ _____

Now go to the Progress Chart to record your score!   Total

Paper 10

Phaeton desperately wanted to drive his father's chariot. He begged Helios, the Greek sun god, to allow him as he wanted to impress his friends on Earth. Phaeton wanted them to believe he was the son of a god. Helios agreed but there was a warning ...

'... whatever you do,' he said sternly, 'do not try to guide the horses. They know the path and, if you do not bother them, they will ride in an arc across the sky, until they reach the safety of the stables in the West.'

He had time to say no more. The great golden courtyard gates swung open. Light began to climb into the dark sky and the restless horses leaped into the waiting blackness.

Helios watched as the wheels and the hooves made splinters of light which surrounded the chariot like a ball of fire.

Phaeton held on tightly to the reins. The chariot thundered into the sky with a speed that made his cloak stream out behind him. The wind lifted his hair and his breath came in gasps.

Gradually, though, he relaxed and he began to enjoy the power and the swiftness of his flight. He looked over the side and thought of the people woken by rays from the sun chariot. He laughed aloud when he thought of the power he had to control people's lives.

'Soon I shall be over my village,' he thought happily, but when he looked over at the ground below him all he could see were patches of grey, brown and green. He was too far away even to see his village, let alone his house.

In despair he cried, 'No one will see that it is me driving the chariot.' He gave the reins an angry tug and steered the great horses away from their path in the sky. Nearer to the Earth they swooped. The stallions gathered speed and hurtled downwards. Too late, Phaeton remembered his father's warning, and he tried desperately to stop the furious flight. The horses, sensing that they were no longer controlled, galloped faster and faster. Their flaming nostrils sent fire licking onto the earth and sparks flew from their hooves. Flames licked buildings, and crops withered and died in the heat. Huge rivers were sucked into the air and only barren, scorched beds remained.

People were in panic. Dust from the parched ground filled their nostrils. Soil crumbled around them. Where were they to turn for help?

Only the father of the gods, Zeus, could help them. Gathering what little they had to offer as gifts, the villagers streamed to his temple and begged for help. Their pitiful cries soon reached the great god and he looked down with amazement at the devastation. He saw the sun chariot racing in great swirls across the sky, the driver hanging on grimly. 30

Taking a thunderbolt, Zeus hurled it with great force at the frightened boy. It hit Phaeton and its power sent him spinning out of the chariot. His body twisted in space until it landed, broken, on the Earth. 35

At a command from Zeus, the horses returned to their proper path. Streaming foam from their bodies made a shimmering haze around them and, as night came, the hidden chariot dissolved into the West and the darkness. 40

From *The Lonely Boy* by Barrie Wade, Ann Wade and Maggie Moore

Underline the correct answers.

1 (Phaeton, Helios, Zeus) is the name of the sun god.

2 Before Phaeton set off on the chariot, Helios warned him to (hold on tight, let the horses guide him, relax and enjoy the ride).

3 What happened to Phaeton when Zeus discovered what he had done? (he was hit by a thunderbolt, he was asked to stop the chariot, he and the chariot were burnt by flames)

Answer these questions.

4 Why was Phaeton keen to drive the chariot?

_____

5–6 Using evidence from the passage, describe Phaeton's character.

_____

_____

_____

_____

7 Copy one line from the passage that shows that the chariot is a **metaphor** for the sun.

_____

_____

_____

8 What does 'barren' mean (line 26)?

_____

9 Write another word for 'scorched'.

_____

10 Describe in your own words the moral of this Greek legend.

_____

_____

_____

_____

Choose the correct **prefix** to complete each word.

    mis   dis   over   re

11 _____act   12 _____count

13 _____charge   14 _____balance

15 _____behave   16 _____touch

17 _____trace   18 _____believe

Rewrite these sentences, adding the missing apostrophes.

19 Bens football had a puncture.

_____

20 They were thirsty, but the cows water trough was empty.

_____

21 It suddenly rained and the three girls coats were soaked.

_____

22 Marks finger hurt after he shut it in a car door!

23 Aunty Sues family waved as they turned the corner.

24 Dan lost his ticket for footballs greatest match, the Cup Final.

25 Five groups designs were displayed in the school hall.

Circle the words that do not have an **antonym**.

26–31 wall   late   London   deep   top   yellow
       careful   diamond   male   month   egg   stay

Rewrite these direct speech sentences into **indirect speech**.

32 'Don't forget that you have homework tonight,' called the teacher.

33 'Where's the nearest toilet?' asked the tourist.

34 'Help, I'm caught in the barbed wire!' screamed the boy.

35 'Stop that ball,' Greg shouted as it was heading for the goal.

36 'I really don't like Mondays,' mumbled Seeta to her best friend.

Use words from the passage to complete the table.

37–48 The chickens had been put away for the night. It had been easy as they had obediently marched to their broken pen, following Jordan as he sneakily tempted them with soggy mashed potato from the evening meal into their home.

noun	pronoun	preposition

Put a *tick* (✓) next to the words spelt correctly and a *cross* (✗) next to those spelt incorrectly.

49 feirce _____   50 diesel _____

51 pier _____   52 conciet _____

53 greivous _____   54 perceive _____

55 viel _____   56 foreign _____

Rewrite the following correctly.

57–71 sashas eyes stared in disbelief standing quietly in a stable was her very own pony i dont believe hes mine she whispered her mother smiled because she knew sasha deserved him

_____

_____

_____

_____

_____

_____

Write the **abbreviations** or **acronyms** of these words.

72 old age pensioner _____

73 centimetre _____

74 Great Britain _____

75 headquarters _____

76 Prime Minister _____

77 personal computer _____

Add an **adjectival phrase** to complete each sentence.

78 Tom washed his hands in the _____ water.

79 Danni kicked her _____ bike.

80 The _____ weather put them off walking.

81 The _____ car broke down once again.

82 Wusai ate the _____ cake hurriedly.

83 Jeremy awoke disturbed after having a _____ nightmare.

Write down three **onomatopoeic** words that can be associated with these.

84–86 thunder

_____   _____   _____

87–89 train station

_____   _____   _____

90–92 swimming pool

_____   _____   _____

Add the **suffix** *ing* to each of these words.

93 hide _____ 94 equip _____

95 picnic _____ 96 amuse _____

97 test _____ 98 enrol _____

99 thief _____ 100 separate _____

Now go to the Progress Chart to record your score! Total ___ 100

Paper 11

After 37 years, polar explorer is brought in from the cold

On April 7 1909 the American explorer Robert Peary, nine months into an Arctic expedition, recorded an ecstatic entry in his diary. 'The Pole at last!!! The prize of three centuries, my dream and ambition for 23 years! *Mine* at last …'

It was not, however, his. He was some distance from the geographic north pole and had not just become the first man to walk on top of the Earth.

Sixty years after Peary's disputed expedition, a young Briton named Wally Herbert led a four-man dogsled team to the pole, as part of an ambitious and still-unrepeated expedition to cross the Arctic Ocean on foot. In so doing, they became the rightful holders of the record that Peary had falsely claimed.

But while Sir Wally, as he became in 1999, may be one of the greatest explorers Britain has produced, he remains relatively unknown outside his field.

'To those that know, he is the man,' the polar explorer Pen Hadow said. 'He is the explorers' explorer, as Sir Ran Fiennes put it.'

In truth, getting to the pole was no more than an incidental ambition for the explorer. On February 21 1968 his party set out from Point Barrow, Alaska, aiming to make the first ever surface crossing of the Arctic Ocean via the north pole. After 15 months on the ice pack – five of them in darkness – the men arrived in Spitzbergen in northern Norway, completing a journey of 3100 km (1926 miles).

'Ice core samples taken by a member of the party have become the benchmark data for all studies into the impact of global warming on the polar ice caps,' Mr Hadow said. 'And that was just one expedition Sir Wally led. He also mapped something like 45,000 square miles, in three areas of the pole. He personally drew the maps, which are still the maps polar explorers use today.'

Taken from an article in *The Guardian* by Esther Addley

Underline the correct answers.

1 What nationality was Robert Peary?

(Norwegian, British, American)

2 In what year did Wally Herbert lead an expedition to the North Pole?

(1968, 1969, 1970)

3 When did Wally Herbert arrive in Norway?

(in daylight hours, in darkness, 15 months after he set out)

Answer these questions.

4 Robert Peary wrote '*Mine* at last …'. What was he referring to?

_____

_____

5 Pick out the phrase from the passage which describes where the North Pole is.

_____

6 What is meant by 'unknown outside his field' on line 12?

_____

_____

7–10 How does the article make is clear that Sir Wally is an explorer worthy of note? Refer to four things from the text in your answer.

_____

_____

_____

_____

Write two **compound words** that begin with these words.

11–12 mean _____ _____

13–14 over _____ _____

15–16 week _____ _____

17–18 fire _____ _____

Use each of these **prepositions** in a sentence of your own.

19 under

_____

20 in

_____

21 along

_____

22–24 List three more **prepositions**.

_____   _____   _____

Copy the passage, adding the missing capital letters.

25–34 having emptied the larder, uncle franklin returned to the rocking chair. he belched loudly, then grinned, trying to make a joke out of it.

mum walked in, in time to hear the burp. 'please frank, don't do that!' she exclaimed. 'isn't it time you were heading home?'

'i've missed the train,' he explained, 'thought i'd stay longer.'

Write a **synonym** for each word in bold.

35 Meena found understanding the computer **jargon** a challenge. _____

36 We are having a **spell** of bad weather. _____

37 I was able to **persuade** my brother to lend me his mp3 player. _____

38 Moving house can be a major **upheaval**. _____

39 The swimmer **plunged** into the pool. _____

40 The head-teacher **seized** his mobile phone. _____

41 Jake **barged** into Henri. _____

42 The radio **broadcast** lasted for three hours. _____

Add a different **conjunction** to complete each sentence.

43 Sam and Tony hesitated at the door _____ they were afraid to enter.

44 Aimee wanted the large bag of sweets _____ she couldn't afford them.

45 Denali had to wait for the doctor _____ he was ready.

46 Jess knows it is recorder practice every Friday _____ she always forgets her recorder.

47 It was raining _____ Mum rushed out to collect the washing.

48 Alice went to Tuhil's house _____ Connor went to Fran's.

Rewrite these sentences without double negatives.

49 There weren't no parking spaces.

_____

50 I wasn't not going to the park.

_____

51 We haven't no money for the fair rides.

_____

52 There isn't no chance we'll make it for the start of the match.

_____

53 Jim hasn't bought no new coat.

_____

Write each of these words in their **singular** form.

54 safes _____   **55** scarves _____

56 deer _____   **57** heroes _____

58 sheep _____   **59** crocuses _____

60 berries _____   **61** shelves _____

Add *was* or *were* in each gap to complete each sentence.

62–63 We _____ waiting for Tony who _____ not ready.

64–65 I _____ asked to play the lead role in the play and Sean _____ chosen to play my brother.

66–67 They _____ worried about the match with Forest School as last year they _____ at the top of the league.

68–69 As you _____ late for the film at the cinema I assume it _____ impossible to get tickets?

Add the **suffix** to each of these words.

70 tasty + er   _____   71 play + ful   _____

72 easy + ly   _____   73 employ + ed   _____

74 spy + ing   _____   75 buy + er   _____

76 beauty + ful   _____   77 merry + ment   _____

Write whether each of these sentences refers to something happening in the **past**, **present** or **future**.

78 I will be going to Disneyland in the summer.   _____

79 We opened our presents quietly.   _____

80 You're eating an apple.   _____

81 He is leaving the house now.   _____

82 The rain will soak the washing on the line.   _____

83 This number challenge is very hard!   _____

84 The clock stopped at 2.30 am.   _____

85 The wind blew the tree down outside our house.   _____

A number of words we use have been 'borrowed' from other languages. Complete the table below, putting the words under the correct country.

86–91 croissant   studio   schnitzel   ravioli   boutique   kindergarten

France	Germany	Italy

Choose the correct **suffix** to turn each **noun** into a **verb**.

en   ise   ify

92 fright _____   93 sign _____

94 solid _____   95 fossil _____

96 glory _____   97 apology _____

Underline the correct word in brackets.

98 He (has, shall) returned the library book on time so won't receive a fine.

99 Rachel (done, did) the dishes after lunch.

100 They (are, was) expected to begin the competition at noon.

Now go to the Progress Chart to record your score!   Total 100

Paper 12

By the shores of Gitche Gumee,
By the shining Big-Sea-Water,
Stood the wigwam of Nokomis,
Daughter of the Moon, Nokomis.
5   Dark behind it rose the forest,
Rose the black and gloomy pine-trees,
Rose the firs with cones upon them;
   There the wrinkled, old Nokomis
Nursed the little Hiawatha,
10 Rocked him in his linden cradle,
Bedded soft in moss and rushes,
Safely bound with reindeer sinews;
Stilled his fretful wail by saying,
'Hush! the Naked Bear will get thee!'
15   Many things Nokomis taught him
Of the stars that shine in heaven;
Showed him Ishkoodah, the comet,
Warriors with their plumes and war-clubs,
Flaring far away to northward
20   At the door on Summer evenings
Sat the little Hiawatha;
Heard the whispering of the pine-trees,
Heard the lapping of the water,
And he sang the song of children,
25 Sang the song Nokomis taught him:

An extract from *The Story of Hiawatha* by H W Longfellow

Underline the correct answers.

1 Where did Nokomis live?

(between a lake and a river, between a river and a forest, between a lake and a forest)

2 Is Nokomis, the daughter of the Moon, a young or old person?

(young, old, poem doesn't state)

Answer these questions.

3 What word in the poem means 'agitated'? _____

4–6 What four things was Hiawatha's cot made of?

_____

_____

_____

_____

7–8 What cultural group do you think this poem is about? Why?

_____

_____

9–10 Nokomis taught Hiawatha many things about the world in which he was growing up. Why do you think that was important?

_____

_____

_____

_____

Each word has a missing silent letter. Rewrite the words correctly.

11 rinocerous _____ **12** buffe _____

13 scrach _____ **14** rasberry _____

15 biscit _____ **16** ristwatch _____

17 eiress _____ **18** sord _____

Write three sentences. One sentence must include brackets, one commas and one dashes to indicate **parenthesis**.

19–20 _____

21–22 _____

23–24 _____

Complete the table below.

25–40 jealousy   Bath Rugby Club   colony   dislike   gaggle   desk
       Iraq   flock   holiday   microscope   Keswick   beauty
       Charlie   puppy   love   bunch

Proper nouns	Abstract nouns	Common nouns	Collective nouns

Write an **onomatopoeic** word for each of the following.

41 a dripping tap   _____

42 a car passing at speed _____

43 a spade digging in mud _____

44 a fire burning   _____

45 thunder   _____

Write a **contraction** for each of these pairs of words.

46 they have _____ 47 there will _____

48 would not _____ 49 shall not _____

50 it is _____ 51 I will _____

52 could have _____ 53 does not _____

Write each of these pairs of short sentences as one sentence, using conjunctions.

54 Monty the dog slept soundly. He was exhausted after his walk.

_____

55 Tariq received his swimming certificate. He swam 30 lengths of the pool.

_____

56 Sophie was very excited. She was having a sleepover at Helen's house.

_____

57 Dan dropped the books he was holding. Meena gave him a fright.

_____

Add the **prefix** *un*, *il* or *im* to each of these words.

58 _____patient 59 _____pleasant

60 _____literate 61 _____interested

62 _____legible 63 _____reliable

64 _____possible 65 _____logical

Rewrite the following correctly.

66–86 what are we going to do? i wailed we are really going to be in trouble this time

only if they catch us replied finn

but they are bound to i mumbled

_____

_____

_____

_____

_____

_____

_____

Write two words for each of the following word classes.

87–88 adjective _____ _____

89–90 pronoun _____ _____

91–92 preposition _____ _____

93–94 conjunction _____ _____

What is the **root word** in each word?

95 thoughtlessness _____   **96** assistance _____

97 possession _____   **98** assembly _____

99 unhelpful _____   **100** computer _____

Now go to the Progress Chart to record your score!   Total / 100

Progress Chart — English 9–10 years Book 2

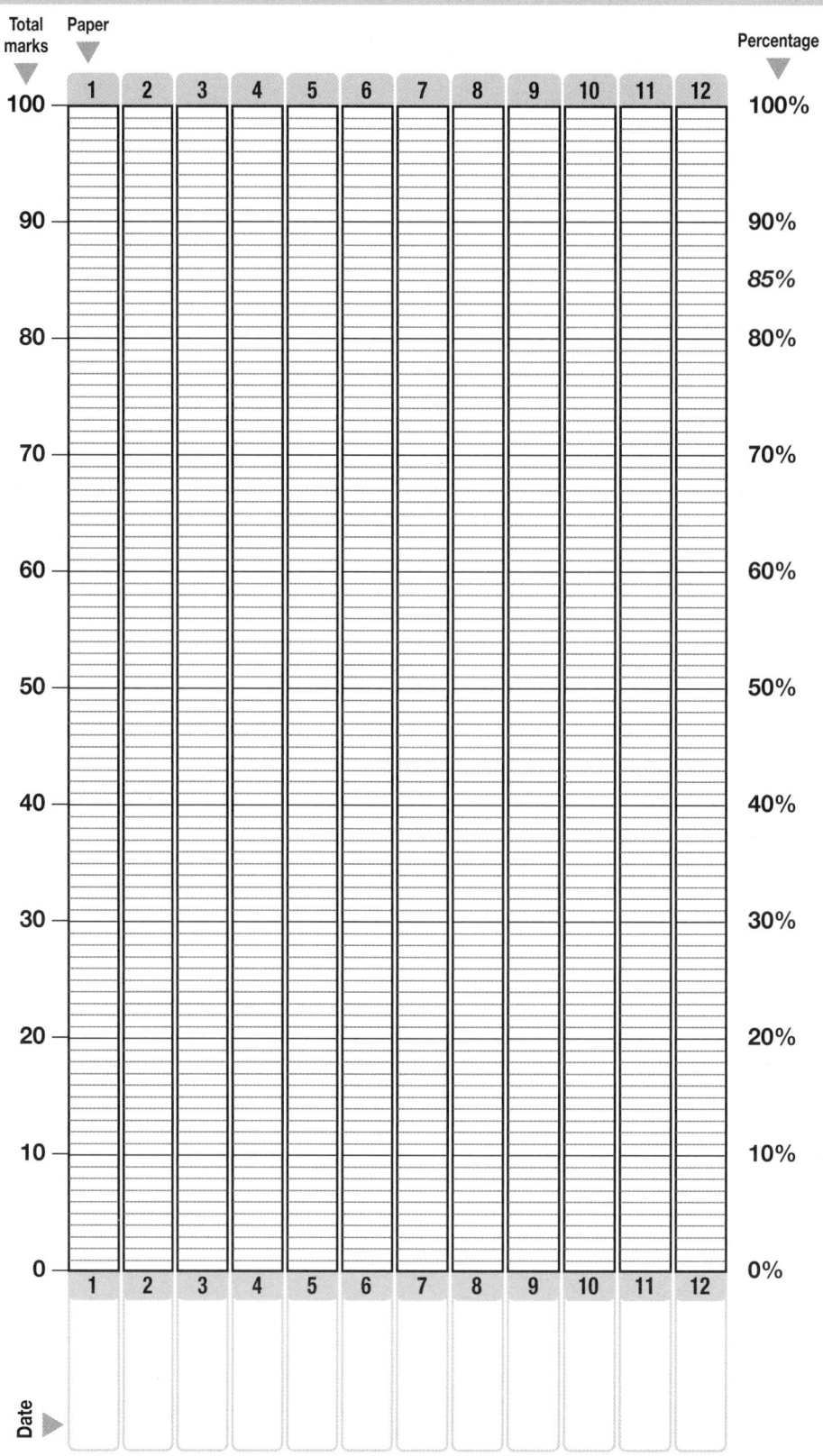

Total marks	Paper 1	2	3	4	5	6	7	8	9	10	11	12	Percentage
100													100%
90													90%
													85%
80													80%
70													70%
60													60%
50													50%
40													40%
30													30%
20													20%
10													10%
0	1	2	3	4	5	6	7	8	9	10	11	12	0%

Date ▶

When you've finished the book use the Next Step Planner ▶